Prayer
Power
and
PROSPERITY

3

KEYS TO A
MOVE OF GOD

Ray Addison

Prayer Power and Prosperity

3

KEYS TO A
MOVE OF GOD

Mark Brazee

MBM Publications
Broken Arrow, Oklahoma

Unless otherwise indicated, all Scripture quotations are taken from the *King James Version* of the Bible.

Prayer, Power, and Prosperity
Second Printing 1998
ISBN 0-93444-05-2
Copyright © 1998 by Mark Brazee Ministries
P. O. Box 1870
Broken Arrow, Oklahoma 74013

Published by MBM Publications
P. O. Box 1870
Broken Arrow, Oklahoma 74013

Table of Contents

Chapter 1
Three Keys to a Move of God

The last days are upon us, and we in the Church are gearing up for God's final harvest and the return of Jesus. God is taking His harvest equipment out of the barns and is changing our "oil" and greasing our "gears" so we will be prepared for what is to come.

Never before has any other generation experienced what we will experience — the greatest move of God the world has ever seen. As the gap between heaven and Earth narrows, and time and eternity move closer and closer together, we will experience the manifested presence of God like never before. In that glory we will see signs, wonders, and miracles. The ministry of angels will be commonplace and people will come to the altar in masses to be saved. The Church is adding the twenty-ninth chapter to the Book of Acts, and then it will be time to go home!

Major Moves of God

If we look through the Bible and compare what the Church is experiencing now to other major moves of God throughout history, we will see a pattern. There are three keys we can identify in major moves of God, both in the Old and New Testaments. When we see momentum building in these three areas in the Body of Christ, we know God is about to accomplish something. God can and does manifest Himself in different ways through individual ministry, local churches, groups of people, or even an entire movement or denomination.

1

But when these three keys start showing up in many groups, flows, nations, and continents, we know we are on the edge of a major move of God, and He is giving the Church the keys to bring it to pass.

God Is in the Key Business

I notice throughout the Bible that God frequently refers to keys. In fact, look at Matthew 16:

> **MATTHEW 16:13-19**
> **13 When Jesus came into the coasts of Caesarea Philippi, he asked his disciples, saying, Whom do men say that I the Son of man am?**
> **14 And they said, Some say that thou art John the Baptist: some, Elias; and others, Jeremias, or one of the prophets.**
> **15 He saith unto them, But whom say ye that I am?**
> **16 And Simon Peter answered and said, Thou art the Christ, the Son of the living God.**
> **17 And Jesus answered and said unto him, Blessed art thou, Simon Barjona: for flesh and blood hath not revealed it unto thee, but my Father which is in heaven.**
> **18 And I say also unto thee, That thou art Peter, and upon this rock I will build my church; and the gates of hell shall not prevail against it.**
> **19 And I will GIVE UNTO THEE THE KEYS of the kingdom of heaven....**

Notice Jesus is talking about building His Church; not only the local church, but the universal Church. He is talking about the plan of God — God's plan *is* the Church.

Along with the reference to building His Church or fulfilling His complete plan on Earth, Jesus said in

Matthew 16:19, "And I will give unto thee the keys of the kingdom of heaven...."

Therefore, in essence Jesus is saying He is going to build the Church that will carry out God's plan on Earth. Then He immediately says, "And I will give unto thee the keys of the kingdom of heaven...." Jesus is giving us the keys we need to fulfill God's plan for the last days.

There are numerous places in the Bible in which Jesus refers to keys. Let's look at two more in the Book of Revelation.

REVELATION 1:18
18 I am he that liveth, and was dead; and, behold, I am alive for evermore, Amen; and have the KEYS of hell and of death.

Jesus also said He had the keys to open doors that no man could shut and to shut doors that no man could open.

REVELATION 3:7
7 ...he that is holy, he that is true, he that HATH THE KEY of David, he that OPENETH, and no man shutteth; and SHUTTETH, and no man openeth.

How does Jesus open and shut those doors? He has the keys! And how does He give us access through those doors? He gives us the keys!

Harvest Doors

The apostle Paul said, "For a great door and effectual is opened unto me..." (1 Corinthians 16:9). Many times we see a door before us, and it seems overwhelming. But we are not waiting for Jesus to come and kick the door open. All we need to open the door is the right key. It doesn't matter how big the door, how heavy the door, how strong the door, or even what is behind the door. If we have the right key, the door will open.

When it comes to going to a particular nation, I have heard people say, "That country is a hard place." Every time I hear someone say that, something rises up from the inside of me, and I want to say, "Just give me a one-way ticket there!"

There is no such thing as a hard place for God, because He has the keys! God has the keys to every city and every nation. He has the keys to open any door He tells us to go through. It doesn't matter how big the door is or how long it has been closed; if we have the right key, that door will open. There are doors that have been closed for a long time, but they are about to open to bring in the last-day harvest. We are not the ones who open the doors; it's the keys! Most of the time it is not the place that is hard; the problem is that no one has bothered to find the right key to get into that place.

I remember when we moved into our first office building. The building had been vacant for a number of years. One day I opened a drawer and found some keys, none of which was marked. I looked around the building. There were doors everywhere, and every door had a lock. I had two handfuls of unmarked keys and no idea which key would open which door. I thought, *If only I could find which key goes where, I would be able to gain access to any room in the building.* I spent some time doing just that, and it worked!

God has the keys to everything He wants to accomplish. It is up to us to find the right key to use for what God wants us to do. How do we find the right key? By spending time in the presence of God. If Jesus has the keys (Revelation 1:18; 3:7), it is through spending time with Him that He will give us those keys. If we want a major move of God, we will have to find the keys to bring it to pass.

The Greatest Move of God

We know there is a major move of God coming. We are right on the edge of miraculous things. There are things God has locked up for us in these last days, but it's going to take the right keys to open them. It's like a safety deposit box at a bank. There are so many valuable things inside, it takes not one but two keys to open it. The move of God that is coming is so great we won't be able to open it with just two keys; it will take three keys. In James 5, we not only see what the next and final move of God is on Earth, but we also see the three keys that will open this move and bring it to pass.

James 5:7,8 actually shows us what the move is:

> **JAMES 5:7,8**
> **7 Be patient therefore, brethren, unto the coming of the Lord. Behold, the husbandman waiteth for the precious fruit of the earth, and hath long patience for it, until he receive the early and latter rain.**
> **8 Be ye also patient; stablish your hearts: for the coming of the Lord draweth nigh.**

What major move are these verses referring to? The return of Jesus! That is the next major move of God. James said we are to be patient unto the coming of the Lord: "...Behold, the husbandman waiteth...." But what is the husbandman waiting for?

He is waiting for the precious fruit of the Earth — the harvest from the seed He planted. This final harvest of souls from all over the Earth will be followed by the return of Jesus.

What will bring in the harvest? Let's look at one of the three major keys to a move of God: *power.*

The Power Key

James 5:7 says, "...Behold, the husbandman waiteth for the precious fruit of the earth, and hath long patience for it, until he receive the early and latter rain."

Hosea 6:3 tells us, "Then shall we know, if we follow on to know the Lord: his going forth is prepared as the morning; and he shall come unto us as the rain, as the latter and former rain unto the earth."

What is rain?

Power.

The Bible says the rain is an outpouring of God Himself. Rain is God coming to Earth; not just in presence, but in power and demonstration. Just as natural rain is the only thing that will cause the seed that has been planted to spring up and produce a harvest, the rain or power of God, spiritually speaking, is the only thing that will produce a harvest of souls.

Every major move of God in history has been marked by power. From the signs and wonders that accompanied the exodus of God's people from Egypt to the 120 in the Upper Room who flooded the streets of Jerusalem boldly speaking in other tongues, power has always been a key to every major move of God, and we will never have a major move of God without it.

The Prayer Key

We know that power is necessary to bring about a major move of God, but there is also another key. What is it that will produce the rain or an outpouring of the Spirit of God? What is it that will produce the power? We find the answer in James 5:13-18:

> **JAMES 5:13-18**
> **13 Is any among you afflicted? let him PRAY. Is any merry? let him sing psalms.**
> **14 Is any sick among you? let him call for the elders of the church; and let them PRAY over him, anointing him with oil in the name of the Lord:**
> **15 And the PRAYER of faith shall save the sick, and the Lord shall raise him up; and if he hath committed sins, they shall be forgiven him.**
> **16 Confess your faults one to another, and PRAY one for another, that ye may be healed. The effectual fervent PRAYER of a righteous man availeth much.**
> **17 Elias was a man subject to like passions as we are, and he PRAYED EARNESTLY that it might not rain: and it rained not on the earth by the space of three years and six months.**
> **18 And he PRAYED AGAIN, and the heaven gave rain, and the earth brought forth her fruit.**

Elijah prayed, and the rain stopped. He prayed again, and the rain started. The prayers of one man caused heaven to rain and the Earth to bring forth fruit. When Elijah prayed, he received physical rain and physical fruit. God is saying if we pray, we will receive spiritual rain and spiritual fruit.

Prayer is a necessary key in every major move of God. James 5:16 (*The Amplified Bible*) says, "...The earnest (heartfelt, continued) prayer of a righteous man makes *tremendous power available* [dynamic in its working]." It is when the Church starts praying with earnest, heartfelt, and continued prayer that tremendous power is made available.

In reading the works of famed missionary John G. Lake, I found that he refers to the praying Church as the generating power of God in the Earth.

One night, Lake was overlooking some villages in South Africa. He counted 1,100 little villages and miles of land within the range of his eyesight. This territory represented millions of people still untouched by the Gospel of Jesus Christ. As Rev. Lake cried out to God about this, he heard the Spirit of the Lord say, "The Church, which is His Body."

After a time, Lake realized this meant that the Church is God's generating power in the Earth — and the only way to generate God's power on Earth is through prayer. It works like electricity. The power is present, but it takes an avenue to channel that power where it is needed. Somewhere down a river there has to be a dynamo that draws electricity out of the air and transmits it over the wires to bring heat, light, and power. Prayer is like God's divine dynamo.

The Prosperity Key

Now let's look at another key, which is found in James 5:1-4:

> **JAMES 5:1-4**
> 1 Go to now, ye rich men, weep and howl for your miseries that shall come upon you.
> 2 Your riches are corrupted, and your garments are motheaten.
> 3 Your gold and silver is cankered; and the rust of them shall be a witness against you, and shall

eat your flesh as it were fire. Ye have heaped
treasure together for the last days.
4 Behold, the hire of the labourers who have
reaped down your fields, which is of you kept
back by fraud, crieth: and the cries of them which
have reaped are entered into the ears of the Lord
of Sabaoth.

The theme throughout the first four verses of this
chapter has to do with the subject of money. We will
deal specifically with this subject later, but for the
present we want to establish that financial prosperity is
one of the three keys to every major move of God. The
Church can have prayer and power, but if there is no
money to take the power to the world, the other two
keys won't do us much good.

Exodus From Egypt

As we study the Bible, we will see the same three
keys exhibited repeatedly in relation to every major
move of God. We will start by looking at the Israelites'
exodus from Egypt.

EXODUS 2:23
23 And it came to pass in process of time, that the
king of Egypt died: and the children of Israel
SIGHED by reason of the bondage, and they
CRIED, and their CRY came up unto God by
reason of the bondage.

Notice the first thing that took place leading to a
major move of God. The people grew tired of their
bondage. They lived with their situation for awhile, but
after about 430 years, they had had enough! The Bible
said they *cried out* to God. Today we would call that

fervent prayer. The children of Israel were ready for
things to change, so they developed a strong prayer life.

What did God do as a result of the cries or *prayers* of
the children of Israel?

God located Moses tending sheep on the backside of
the desert and spoke to him out of a burning bush.

> **EXODUS 3:7**
> 7 And the Lord said, I have surely seen the
> affliction of my people which are in Egypt, and
> have HEARD THEIR CRY by reason of their
> taskmasters; for I know their sorrows.

In response to the prayers of the children of Israel,
God sent Moses to deliver His people from the bondage
of Egypt.

Speaking to Moses in Exodus 3:19,20, God said:

> **EXODUS 3:19,20**
> 19 And I am sure that the king of Egypt will not
> let you go, no, not by a mighty hand.
> 20 And I WILL STRETCH OUT MY HAND, and
> smite Egypt with all my WONDERS which I will
> do in the midst thereof: and after that he will let
> you go.

God told Moses that the king of Egypt would not let
the children of Israel go until He stretched out His
hand and smote Egypt with wonders. When God starts
doing wonders, the result will be an outpouring of
power. It took a mighty show of signs and wonders to
bring about a major move of God in Egypt. What was
the result of this outpouring of power?

> **EXODUS 3:21,22**
> 21 And I will give this people FAVOUR in the sight
> of the Egyptians: and it shall come to pass, that,
> when ye go, ye shall NOT GO EMPTY:

**22 But every woman shall borrow of her neigh-
bour, and of her that sojourneth in her house,
JEWELS OF SILVER, and JEWELS OF GOLD, and
RAIMENT: and ye shall put them upon your sons,
and upon your daughters; and YE SHALL SPOIL
the Egyptians.**

The children of Israel came out of the bondage of
Egypt with great substance: jewels of silver, jewels of
gold, and raiment. Great prosperity flooded God's
people as they were brought out of Egypt.

Prosperity is another of the three keys necessary to
every major move of God. The children of Israel cried
out to God for a change in their situation. They
experienced the power of God in a mighty demonstration
of signs and wonders. Then they left Egypt with great
substance. *The children of Israel went from prayer to
power to prosperity.*

Praying Down the Power of God

We notice the same three keys — prayer, power, and
prosperity — in the New Testament; particularly in the
Book of Acts. Acts is a blueprint for the last days of the
Church. It gives us a picture of what we can expect in
the latter rain, the last great outpouring of God's Spirit.

In Acts 1, the Early Church was ready for an
outpouring of the Holy Ghost. What did those first
Christians do? They went to the Upper Room and
prayed (Acts 1:14). Then, in Acts 2:1-4:

ACTS 2:1-4
**1 And when the day of Pentecost was fully come,
they were all with one accord in one place.**

2 And suddenly there came a sound from heaven as of a rushing mighty wind, and it filled all the house where they were sitting.
3 And there appeared unto them cloven tongues like as of fire, and it sat upon each of them.
4 And they were all filled with the Holy Ghost, and began to speak with other tongues, as the Spirit gave them utterance.

On the Day of Pentecost, the Church prayed the power down. It always takes prayer to *bring* God's power, and it takes prayer to *maintain* that power.

The Early Church knew how to keep the power in operation. Look at Acts 2:42: "And they continued stedfastly in the apostles' doctrine and fellowship, and in breaking of bread, and in prayers." They stayed in the Word, *and* they prayed. What happened next is found in the next verse:

ACTS 2:43
43 And fear came upon every soul: and MANY WONDERS AND SIGNS were done by the apostles.

The Church was praying, and soon they had wonders and signs — or *power*. We will never have a major move of God without power, and we will never have a major move of God without prayer.

ACTS 2:44,45
44 And all that believed were together, and had all things common;
45 And SOLD THEIR POSSESSIONS AND GOODS, and parted them to all men, AS EVERY MAN HAD NEED.

A "spirit of liberality" was produced in the Church, and we will look at the fruit of it later. Where there is liberality or giving, there will always be prosperity.

The Church prayed down the power, and along with the power came a flood of finances or *prosperity*. As a result of these three keys — prayer, power, and prosperity — "...the Lord added to the church daily such as should be saved" (Acts 2:47). This is the same way we're going to reach the nations today. Prayer will produce the power and bring in the prosperity it will take to get the message of the Gospel to the nations.

Prayer Brings Signs and Wonders

Let's look at another example of these three keys in Acts 4. The man at the Gate Beautiful had just been raised up, and consequently Peter and John were commanded by the authorities to preach no more in the name of Jesus.

> **ACTS 4:23,24**
> **23 And being let go, they went to their own company, and reported all that the chief priests and elders had said unto them.**
> **24 And when they heard that, THEY LIFTED UP THEIR VOICE to God with one accord....**

In other words, Peter and John came to their own company and *prayed*. Look what happened as a result of their prayers:

> **ACTS 4:29-31**
> **29 And now, Lord, behold their threatenings: and grant unto thy servants, that with all BOLDNESS they may speak thy word,**
> **30 By stretching forth thine hand to heal; and that SIGNS AND WONDERS may be done by the name of thy holy child Jesus.**
> **31 And when they had PRAYED, THE PLACE WAS SHAKEN where they were assembled together;**

**and they were all filled with the Holy Ghost, and
they spake the word of God with BOLDNESS.**

When the Early Church prayed, the power of God
manifested in the form of signs and wonders. What was
the result?

> **ACTS 4:32-35**
> **32 And the multitude of them that believed were
> of one heart and of one soul: neither said any of
> them that ought of the things which he possessed
> was his own; but they had all things common.**
> **33 And with GREAT POWER gave the apostles
> witness of the resurrection of the Lord Jesus: and
> great grace was upon them all.**
> **34 Neither was there ANY AMONG THEM THAT
> LACKED: for as many as were possessors of lands
> or houses sold them, and BROUGHT THE PRICES
> of the things that were sold,**
> **35 And laid them down at the apostles' feet: and
> distribution was made UNTO EVERY MAN
> ACCORDING AS HE HAD NEED.**

The Word of God was being preached in power, and
verse 34 says, "Neither was there any among them that
lacked...." Why? Because prosperity began to flow in the
Church.

Verse 32 says a multitude of people believed. We
don't know exactly how many make up a "multitude,"
but we do know there were 120 in the Upper Room,
3,000 were added on the Day of Pentecost, and 5,000
were added in the Temple following the healing of the
man at the Gate Beautiful. That adds up to a minimum
of 8,120 believers, none of whom lacked. A church of
more than 8,000 members with no one lacking is a very
prosperous church!

The first outpouring of rain in the New Testament came in the Book of Acts after the 120 prayed. Then when the apostles prayed with their own company in Acts 4, we find signs, wonders, and such a flood of finances that no one lacked. If abundance flowed through the Church in the early rain, I am convinced we will see it in the latter rain!

God's Spirit Poured Out on the Gentiles

There was another major move of God in Acts 10. Here God was looking for a channel through whom to pour out His Spirit upon the Gentiles.

ACTS 10:1,2
1 There was a certain man in Caesarea called Cornelius, a centurion of the band called the Italian band,
2 A devout man, and one that feared God with all his house, WHICH GAVE MUCH ALMS to the people, AND PRAYED to God alway.

When God looks for people upon whom to pour out His Spirit, He looks for those people who *pray* and *give.* Why? Because He knows people like that will keep the power prayed down and will funnel the finances to take the Gospel to the world. We can see through this passage that Cornelius was both a pray-er and a giver. God was looking for a place to pour out the Holy Ghost, and He found just the location.

In the meantime, God confirmed to Peter in a vision that he was to take the Gospel to the Gentile world. Cornelius sent three of his men to Joppa to find Peter and bring him back to Caesarea to speak to the Gentiles.

Acts 10:44-46
**44 While Peter yet spake these words, the Holy
Ghost fell on all them which heard the word.**
**45 And they of the circumcision which believed
were astonished, as many as came with Peter,
because that on the Gentiles also was poured out
the gift of the Holy Ghost.**
**46 For they heard them speak with tongues, and
magnify God....**

This move of God began with *prayer* and *prosperity*,
and then proceeded with a mighty demonstration of
power. We are beginning to see a pattern. It is so
important for us to recognize these three keys, because
they are a blueprint for the move of God in these last
days.

Three Keys Working Together

To accomplish the job of bringing in the end-time
harvest, it will take the three keys of prayer, power, and
prosperity working together. Just as there can be no
electricity in a building without a dynamo or generator
to produce that power, there can be no power without
prayer to produce it. The combination of the two will
produce a wonderful move of God in the Church.
However, if God says, "Take this move to the nations,"
but we can't afford to do it, we will abort God's ultimate
plan.

When God pours out a major move, it is not meant
for just one church, one city, one state, or one nation; it
is meant to touch the world. God has a much greater
purpose in mind than simply to bless you or me; His
plan is to get the Church praying so He can demonstrate
His power and flood the Church with the finances

needed to take this move to every kindred, tongue, people, and nation!

It will take a great influx of finances coming into the Church to pay for this move. As someone said, "The Gospel is free; it is the pipes to get the Gospel where it needs to go that cost money."

It will take all three keys working together to bring about the next and greatest move of God!

Chapter 2
Saving for a Rainy Day

James 5 gives us a picture of the last great outpouring of the Spirit of God upon the Earth. James, writing by inspiration of the Holy Ghost, shows us where we are in time and relation to the return of Jesus.

God does things in "times." In Galatians 4:4, we find that God brought forth His Son in the *fullness* of time.

There was also a set time for the Holy Ghost to fall. Acts 2:1 says, "And when the day of Pentecost was fully come, they were all with one accord in one place." There is no time frame on individual blessings like being saved, healed, or prospered, when it comes to individual blessings, it is always "whosoever will, let him come." But for end-time events, such as moves of God, revivals, or outpourings, there are set times.

Using James 5:7,8 as the focal point of that chapter, we can locate where we are now in time.

> **JAMES 5:7,8**
> **7 Be patient therefore, brethren, unto the coming of the Lord. Behold, the husbandman waiteth for the precious fruit of the earth, and hath long patience for it, until he receive the early and latter rain.**
> **8 Be ye also patient; stablish your hearts: for THE COMING OF THE LORD DRAWETH NIGH.**

Jesus is coming soon! James is showing us there are keys necessary for the Church to have before Jesus returns. He says, "...Behold, the husbandman waiteth for the precious fruit of the earth, and hath long patience for it, until he receive the early and the latter rain."

19

We referred to the rain or an outpouring of God's power, and we referred to prayer, the dynamo that will bring about the power. When we pray for the rain, we are praying for the power that will bring in the harvest.

But we also saw a third key to focus on, and that is prosperity, or the money necessary to finance the harvest.

The Church seems to have had some revelation of the need for the power of God in demonstration and manifestation to bring about a major move of God. We have also had some revelation of the importance of prayer to bring about a major move of God. We will never have a major move of God without these two keys. But the key that seems to have been missing is prosperity.

We have had a group on one side called the "fivefold ministry," and we have had a group on the other side called "the lost." We have the group with the message, holding what the world needs, on one side. Then we have the world on the other side needing what those in the ministry have.

Between the two groups there is a great gulf, and it has been difficult to go from one place to the other. We have needed a bridge between the two groups, but the bridge has been missing. What is the major tool that has kept the Church from reaching the world? Money.

On one hand, the world has looked at the Church and thought, *I've got it bad enough now; I don't want to go over to the Church and be broke.* On the other hand, the Church has looked at the world and said, "If you have money you can't get in, because you are supposed to be poor." We have had revelation on the key of prayer. We have had revelation on the key of power. But revelation concerning the key of prosperity has been sorely lacking.

A man in his late fifties walked up to me at a recent meeting and said, "I went to Bible school when I was younger. God spoke to me there, and I knew He called me to a particular nation."

"Did you ever go?" I asked.

He said, "I never had the money."

This man had a call to a nation, but there was one key missing: money.

On one hand we have a man saying he has a call to missions, but he cannot go because he doesn't have the money. On the other hand, we have the Church saying, "Money is wrong."

The Purpose of Prosperity

Apparently, if we are ever to reach the world, something has change. Prosperity is the key the Church must grasp if we are to reach the world. If we start with the basis of *why* God wants us to be prosperous, people will be more willing to accept it. The purpose is the world. The purpose is not to see how many "toys" we can accumulate. Prosperity isn't gauged by what we *have*; it is gauged by what we *give*. So the prosperity key is the one we have needed to open this last and greatest move of God. We see this key in James 5:1: "Go to now, ye rich men, weep and howl for your miseries that shall come upon you." It is evident that James is referring to money. Some read that verse and say, "God is pronouncing woes on rich people, so it must be wrong to be rich."

Paul told Timothy in Second Timothy 2:15, "Study to shew thyself approved unto God, a workman that needeth not to be ashamed, rightly dividing the word of truth." We wouldn't have to be told to *rightly* divide the Word of truth unless it was possible to *wrongly* divide it. What has happened is that the Church has taken the Word of truth and wrongly divided it, and we ended up with the wrong message. If we rightly divide the Word, that means we are going to study other verses until we get the right perspective on it. If James is referring to "rich," it would be helpful to study further and see what else the Bible has to say about the word "rich."

> **2 CORINTHIANS 8:9**
> **9   For ye know the GRACE of our Lord Jesus Christ, that, though he was RICH, yet for your sakes he became poor, that ye THROUGH HIS POVERTY might be RICH.**

Rich can't be wrong, because the Bible said Jesus made us rich. Jesus became poor, but not for God's benefit or for His own sake. He didn't do it for the angels, the cherubim, or the seraphim. The Bible said Jesus became poor for *our sakes*. Jesus didn't become poor because it was wrong to be rich; He became poor to take our place. Everything Jesus did for us was substitutionary. He took our sins because sin isn't God's plan for us. He took our sickness for the same reason. Then He became poor for us because, again, poverty is not God's plan for man.

Divine Exchange

We could say everything Jesus did for us was a divine exchange. Jesus took our sickness to give us His health. He took our sin to give us His righteousness. He took our separation from God to give us His relationship with God. Jesus took everything we were and made us everything He is. Through His death, burial, resurrection, and ascension to the Father's right hand, Jesus made sure we would be abundantly supplied.

The blood Jesus shed to save us is the same blood He shed to heal and prosper us. Prosperity is a blessing of redemption that was paid for by the precious blood of the Lord Jesus Christ. As far as God is concerned, the minute we were born again, not only were we saved, but we were also made healthy and prosperous.

If rich is wrong, we are all in trouble, because the Bible says we are all rich.

Someone may say, "Well, I don't feel rich."

Sometimes we don't feel healed either, but that doesn't change the fact that we are healed (Isaiah 53:4,5; 1 Peter 2:24).

The blessings of redemption legally belong to every born-again, blood-bought child of God. Many people never walk in the baptism of the Holy Ghost, never walk in divine health, and never walk in the wisdom of God or the joy of the Lord but that doesn't change the fact that those blessings have been purchased for them. The blessings of prosperity belong to us whether we walk in them or not, because the price has been paid for us to be prosperous. Remember, Jesus became poor for our sakes.

I've heard people say, "Brother, you've got to understand that's talking about being spiritually poor — Jesus was made *spiritually* poor."

Anyone who heals the sick, cleanses the leper, and raises the dead could not be spiritually poor! When Jesus came to this Earth, He took on a flesh-and-blood body. He laid aside His omnipotence, omniscience, and omnipresence. Before that time, He was all-knowing and all-powerful and could be everywhere at one time. But He stripped Himself of His mighty power and glory when He left the throne of God.

> **PHILIPPIANS 2:5-7**
> **5 Let this mind be in you, which was also in Christ Jesus:**
> **6 Who, being in the form of God, thought it not robbery to be equal with God:**
> **7 But made himself of no reputation, and TOOK UPON HIM THE FORM OF A SERVANT, and was made in the likeness of men.**

Jesus humbled Himself and became like us. He lived on streets of gold in heaven where gates are made of pearl. Jesus' poverty was not determined by what He had on Earth; it was determined by what He left behind to come to Earth. Even if Jesus had lived in the biggest mansion on the highest hill while on Earth, it would still have seemed poor in comparison to what He left in heaven.

With that in mind, Jesus could not have been made spiritually poor. It must mean that He was made *materially* poor. When we say Jesus was made "poor," we still have to qualify that statement.

It does not mean Jesus lived in abject poverty. Jesus may have been made poor, but God still took care of Him. Jesus never had to hitchhike around the Sea of Galilee. And Judas was caught embezzling from the money bag. If someone could sneak something *out* of the bag, there must have been something *in* the bag to begin with. In Luke 8, we see three persons among others who ministered to Jesus of their substance.

I like one person in particular who is named in Luke 8:3: "And Johanna the wife of Chuza Herod's steward, and Susanna, and many others, which ministered unto him of their substance." Johanna was the wife of Chuza, who just happened to be Herod's steward. Who was Herod? Herod was the king! This means Jesus was supported financially by a partner who was married to the man who handled the king's money!

So apparently Jesus didn't have to "wander like a beggar through the heat and the cold." But when we think of the price He paid to come to Earth and set us free, we can see that for our sakes He was made poor *materially*, that we through His poverty might be made rich.

According to Your Faith

That brings up another question. What is "rich"? The Bible doesn't give us a specific definition of "rich." Why? Because God leaves it up to us. To one person, "rich" is to come to the end of the month and have every bill paid. These persons don't have any money left, and they finish up the month with a zero balance. The next person may say, "I want to finish up the month and still have $10 left. To me that is rich."

Another person will say, "I want to be able to pay all my bills, support 20 ministries, and have $100 left at the end of the month."

Someone else's definition of "rich," may be to have an unlimited checking account so that when a missionary or an ambassador to a nation needs a vehicle, all he has to ask is, "What color, what kind, and how many do you need?"

The Bible doesn't give us a definition of "rich" because we determine our lifestyle. It is set by us, not by God.

In the Book of Matthew, for example, there were two blind men crying out for the mercy of God, desiring to be healed. Jesus was "locating" these blind men in Matthew 9:28 when He asked them, "...Believe ye that I am able to do this? They said unto him, Yea, Lord." Jesus made a strong statement in the next verse when He said, "...According to your faith be it unto you" (verse 29). Jesus touched their eyes, and they were opened (verse 30). It was the faith of the blind men that moved Jesus to heal them.

But it is not simply the fact that we believe God that will cause Him to move. It also has to do with "where" we believe God, or at what level we believe Him. We are the determining factor.

There are different levels of faith. The Bible talks about *great* faith, *weak* faith, *strong* faith, and *shipwrecked* faith, to name a few. God is saying that He will meet us on whatever level of faith we decide to operate.

In Mark 5, we find a man named Jairus, who was operating on a particular level of faith. Jesus was walking through a crowd, and Jairus, the ruler of the synagogue, came to Him and said, "...My little daughter lieth at the point of death: I pray thee, come and lay thy hands on her, that she may be healed; and she shall live" (verse 23).

Where was Jairus' faith? Jairus believed if Jesus would come and lay His hands on his daughter, she would be healed and live. Jesus left the crowd and went with Jairus to the house where the little girl lay. However, when they arrived, the child was already dead. Jesus said, "...the damsel is not dead, but sleepeth" (verse 39).

The people laughed Jesus to scorn (verse 40). They didn't believe. But Jairus did — and he received *exactly* what he believed and said. "And he [Jesus] took the damsel by the hand, and said unto her, Talitha cumi; which is, being interpreted, Damsel, I say unto thee, arise. And straightway the damsel arose, and walked; for she was of the age of twelve years. And they were astonished with a great astonishment" (verses 41,42).

Levels of Faith

We see a second level of faith in Mark 5:25-34:

MARK 5:25-34
25 And a certain woman, which had an issue of blood twelve years,
26 And had suffered many things of many physicians, and had spent all that she had, and was nothing bettered, but rather grew worse,
27 When she had heard of Jesus, CAME IN THE PRESS BEHIND, AND TOUCHED HIS GARMENT.
28 FOR SHE SAID, IF I MAY TOUCH BUT HIS CLOTHES, I SHALL BE WHOLE.
29 And straightway the fountain of her blood was dried up; and she felt in her body that she was healed of that plague.
30 And Jesus, immediately knowing in himself that virtue had gone out of him, turned him about in the press, and said, Who touched my clothes?
31 And his disciples said unto him, Thou seest the multitude thronging thee, and sayest thou, Who touched me?
32 And he looked round about to see her that had done this thing.
33 But the woman fearing and trembling, knowing what was done in her, came and fell down before him, and told him all the truth.
34 And he said unto her, Daughter, THY FAITH hath made thee whole; go in peace, and be whole of thy plague.

Notice the woman said, "If I may touch his clothes, I shall be whole." That is where the woman's faith was located. She came through the crowd behind Jesus, touched His garment, and power flowed out of Him. Jesus didn't walk up to her and deliver her. He didn't lay His hands on her. He didn't even see her.

But He knew someone had touched Him with a different touch! It wasn't a needful touch or a hopeful touch. The woman touched Jesus with *a touch of faith*, and it caused healing power to flow out of Him and into her. What did Jesus say to the woman when He saw who it was who had touched Him? He told her, "...Daughter, *thy faith* hath made thee whole...."

In Matthew 8, we find another level of faith. A centurion came to Jesus on behalf of his servant and said, "...Lord, my servant lieth at home sick of the palsy, grievously tormented" (verse 6). Jesus answered, "...I will come and heal him." But the centurion said, "...Lord, I am not worthy that thou shouldest come under my roof: but speak the word only, and my servant shall be healed. For I am a man under authority, having soldiers under me: and I say to this man, Go, and he goeth; and to another, Come, and he cometh; and to my servant, Do this, and he doeth it" (Matthew 8:8,9).

Jesus told the centurion, "...Verily I say unto you, I have not found so great faith, no, not in Israel" (verse 10). Apparently *great faith* is one level of faith. With great faith, we take the Word, believe it, and go our way. Jesus turned to the centurion and said, "...Go thy way; and as thou hast believed, so be it done unto thee. And his servant was healed in the selfsame hour" (Matthew 8:13).

We have three examples: First, Jairus, who said, "If you come and lay your hands on my daughter, she will be healed and live." Then we have the woman with the issue of blood, who said, "If I may just touch His clothes, I will be whole." Last, the centurion, who said, "If you just speak the Word, my servant will be healed." All three received exactly *what they believed*.

There are levels of faith, and whatever level of faith we decide to apply, Jesus will meet us there. God is no respecter of persons. Faith will work the same for anyone who will believe. According to our faith, so be it unto us. The choice is up to us!

Abundant Supply

That is why God leaves "rich" up to us. That word "rich" may not mean a $1 billion bank account, but it does mean *an abundant supply*. One billion dollars could be lost overnight, but if we have an abundant supply, anything lost would show up again the next day. *Abundance means the money is there when we need it.*

God didn't decide to give us all $1 million and say, "Now you are set for the rest of your life." Most people would lose $1 million in a short period of time. Instead of giving us $1 million and saying, "Do whatever you want with this money," God decided to take care of us throughout our lives. He decided to give us *an abundant supply*! If Jesus was made poor so we could be made rich or abundantly supplied, it must not be wrong to be rich. We have established the fact that Jesus made us all rich. So if God is pronouncing woes on the rich, James 5:1 must be referring to the rich in the world, not to those in the Church.

The Bible never said it is wrong to be rich. In fact, Paul wrote in First Timothy, "Charge them that are rich in this world, that they be not highminded, nor trust in uncertain riches, but in the living God, who giveth us richly all things to enjoy; That they do good, that they be rich in good works, ready to distribute, willing to communicate" (1 Timothy 6:17,18). Paul wasn't saying it is wrong to be rich; he was giving the rich instructions concerning their lifestyle.

I have heard people ask, "But what about Matthew 19:24?" That verse reads, "And again I say unto you, It is easier for a camel to go through the eye of a needle, than for a rich man to enter into the kingdom of God."

History tells us "the eye of a needle" refers to an entrance into a city. Usually, the entrance was built low to the ground. Thus, the only way a camel could get into the city was to get on its knees. In comparison, the only way for a rich man to enter the kingdom of heaven is on his knees! God never said the rich couldn't enter the kingdom of heaven; nor did He say we couldn't be rich in the kingdom. He just said it would be more difficult for the rich to enter, because often the rich trust in their own riches. The Bible says we can't trust in riches to get us into heaven. We must humble ourselves and come in through God's mercy and grace.

Is God upset because people in the world are rich? No. Money doesn't bother God. Then why is God pronouncing woes on the rich in the world?

JAMES 5:1-3
1   Go to now, ye rich men, weep and howl for your miseries that shall come upon you.
2   Your RICHES are CORRUPTED, and your GARMENTS are MOTHEATEN.

3   Your GOLD and SILVER is CANKERED; and the rust of them shall be a witness against you, and shall eat your flesh as it were fire. Ye have HEAPED TREASURE together for the LAST DAYS.

The Amplified Bible says it this way: "Your abundant wealth has rotted and is ruined, and your [many] garments have become moth-eaten. Your gold and silver are completely rusted through, and their rust will be testimony against you and it will devour your flesh as if it were fire. You have heaped together treasure for the last days." Things don't rust when they are moving; they rust when they are sitting. The only reason the gold would be rusted through is because it has been sitting too long doing nothing. God is not pronouncing woes on the rich in this world because they have money. He is pronouncing woes on the rich in this world because they have been hoarding up the money, and God has another purpose for it.

The world has been heaping treasures together for their last days — for themselves, their children, their grandchildren, and their great-grandchildren. And the Bible says their silver, their gold, and their raiment have been sitting there so long doing nothing, they have completely rusted through. These treasures have been hoarded up for generations. What the world doesn't realize is that the treasures they are heaping together for *their* last days are the treasures reserved for *the* last days!

For years, people in the world have been "putting money away." They say they are saving for "a rainy day." Often our response to those people is to laugh and say, "If you save for a rainy day, you'll get one." But there is an "up" side to that statement. The world has been saving for years for a rainy day — and it is starting to rain!

The Church has been praying for the rain, spiritually speaking, and this is the time of the latter rain. The world has been saving for a rainy day — they just didn't know it was Holy Ghost rain! It's starting to rain, and what the world has been saving for 6,000 years is going to be transferred into the kingdom of God.

Money Talks

James says the money the world has been stockpiling for so many years is starting to do something.

> **JAMES 5:4**
> **4 Behold, the hire of the labourers who have reaped down your fields, which is of you kept back by fraud, CRIETH: and the cries of them which have reaped are entered into the ears of the Lord of Sabaoth.**

James says the money is crying out to God. It is scriptural for money to cry out. The blood of Abel cried out, "...the voice of thy brother's blood *crieth* unto me from the ground" (Genesis 4:10). And Jesus said in Luke 19:40 that if we don't praise Him, the rocks will cry out.

The blood of Jesus is still speaking. Hebrews 12:24 says, "And to Jesus the mediator of the new covenant, and to the blood of sprinkling, that *speaketh* better things than that of Abel."

The world has said for years, "When money talks, we listen." Well, money is talking, and this time it is saying, "I am in the wrong place! I am supposed to be reaching lives. I am not supposed to be stored up in the world's stocks, bonds, CDs, and money markets! I'm in the wrong place!"

If we back up a little, we will see not only is James talking about money; he is talking about the hire or the wages of the laborers for whom this money is destined.

JAMES 5:4
4 Behold, the HIRE OF THE LABOURERS who have reaped down your fields, which is of you KEPT BACK BY FRAUD....

James says the hire or the wages belong to the laborers who work in the harvest fields. We need to define what James means by "laborers." In the Gospels, Jesus refers to those who work in the harvest fields as "laborers." In John 4:34-36, Jesus was teaching His disciples about finishing His work:

JOHN 4:34-36
34 Jesus saith unto them, My meat is to do the will of him that sent me, and to finish his work.

We know the will of God is redemption — the death, burial, and resurrection of Jesus. That is the will of God, but what is meant by "finish His work"?

35 Say not ye, There are yet four months, and then cometh harvest? behold, I say unto you, Lift up your eyes, and look on the fields; for they are white already to harvest.

The plan of redemption is the will of God. Finishing that plan is bringing in the harvest. Harvest is the "finishing" part of the redemptive plan.

36 And HE THAT REAPETH RECEIVETH WAGES, AND GATHERETH FRUIT UNTO LIFE ETERNAL: that both he that soweth and he that reapeth may rejoice together.

Reapers work in the harvest fields, and the Bible says that those who work in those fields are going to receive wages. The money isn't going just to the Church, but to those who are working in the fields. The wages are going to be poured out during harvest! God has been saving for a rainy day, and when it starts to rain, He is going to turn the money loose. When that happens, the laborers in the harvest fields will start to receive paychecks as they do their appointed jobs.

The Tool Not the Goal

For the last 6,000 years, the money has been crying out, "I'm in the wrong place!" At the same time, the Church has been crying, "Money is wrong. It's a sin to have it." So God has had to wait for a new breed who will take Him at His word and realize money is not a goal; it's a tool. It isn't money that is evil; it's what some people have done with it that is evil.

If money is our goal, we are in trouble, because our motive is wrong. Money is not the goal; it is a tool to get to the goal. For example, a man could be building a house because he is a carpenter by trade. That doesn't mean he should go to the hardware store and buy 15 hammers, hang them on the wall, and bow down to them every morning. He doesn't say, "If I can build four houses, I can get eight hammers."

His goal isn't to see how many hammers he can acquire. His goal is to get his hands on a hammer so he can build a house. Our goal is not to see how much money we can bring in. Our objective should be, "Look how much we can do with the money that comes in." Money is just a tool. It is not an object to be worshipped or coveted.

I remember hearing a story about a well-known evangelist, and this story has always stayed with me. He was holding a meeting, and after one of the services he called a staff meeting and told them, "We are not meeting our budget. The money just isn't coming in."

But he never said, "What can we do to get the money in?" Instead, he said, "Where are we not meeting the people's needs?"

They made some adjustments, and the money came in. But the money was not the goal; it was just a tool.

Harvest Account

God has all the tools needed by those who will work in His fields. In fact, God has a huge harvest account waiting to be used to reach the lost and bring in the harvest in the last days. If God has a special account set up to do a special job, who do you suppose is going to get the account? The laborers. Who are laborers? Those who are working in God's harvest fields gathering fruit to life eternal.

God knows the end from the beginning. The Book of Ezekiel makes reference to "a wheel in the middle of a wheel" (Ezekiel 1:16). Take a bicycle wheel, for example. We have the outside part, and we have the inside or hub part. Picture God sitting in the middle of the wheel, or eternity. We are in the outside rim, or time. There are thousands of spokes going from one point to another. God can look down a spoke in one place and see creation. He can look down a spoke in another place and see the Red Sea being split. He can look any direction and see ahead to any period in time. God can sit in one spot and see past, present, and future all at once. God is not limited by time, because He is in eternity. That is how He looked ahead to Adam's fall, backed up before creation, and set redemption into motion.

We can see redemption, God's plan for man, in the Garden of Eden. Man had sonship, fellowship, health, and prosperity. Every need man had was abundantly supplied there. God looked ahead and saw man fall, losing all his God-given benefits, and God knew He must provide a redeemer for man.

God looked back in time and put His plan of redemption into motion by calling Jesus "...the Lamb slain from the foundation of the world" (Revelation 13:8). Before Adam ever fell, God had a plan to redeem mankind. From the foundation of the world, God knew He would send Jesus.

Then God looked farther down the road and saw there would be a great harvest of souls near the end of time — the harvest from the seed He planted called Jesus Christ (Hebrews 2:9,10).

He also knew when it came time for His Church to bring in the harvest, it would cost a great deal of money. God couldn't rain down money from heaven, or He would be a counterfeiter. So while Earth was still in His possession, God planted a "harvest account" here. God put something in the Earth that would serve as the financial standard from now until the return of Jesus. He planted gold, and the first thing He did was show Adam where it was buried (Genesis 2:11,12). Why did God choose gold? Because gold is accepted in any country and in any currency.

Pools of Wealth

We could compare the reserves of money to the oil that is buried under the Earth's surface. There were pools of oil under the surface of the Earth for a long time before we ever had a need for oil and discovered it would run automobiles and airplanes and help transport us all over the world with the Gospel. Once we found out what oil was and what it could be used for, we tapped into those reserves.

Haggai 2:9 says, "The glory of this latter house shall be greater than of the former...." Everything God needs to finance the building of His kingdom has already been placed in the Earth. He said His last-day move will be more glorious than the first. If Acts 2 shows us the *first* days, can you imagine the *last* days?

Let's go back one verse to Haggai 2:8: "The silver is mine, and the gold is mine, saith the Lord of hosts." I had always wondered why those two verses were written back-to-back. The prophet is saying that a move of God is coming that will be greater than anything we have ever seen. It is going to cost a lot of money to pay for this move, but it is God's move, and He can afford it. The silver and the gold are the Lord's, and they are already in the Earth. The fullness of the Earth belongs to God! (See First Corinthians 10:26.)

Just as oil is found under the surface of the Earth, pools of wealth are buried in the Earth, spiritually speaking. The wealth has been in the world system, kept there by God for the last days, when the Church would need to access it. And regardless of what anyone says, there is more than enough money to finance the coming move of God.

A recent newspaper article stated that since the printing of $1 bills began, there have been 62 $100 bills printed for every $1 bill that has been printed. There is no shortage of money.

This Gospel of the Kingdom

The last major move of God we will see is predicted in Matthew 24:14: "And this gospel of the kingdom shall be preached in all the world for a witness unto all nations; and then shall the end come." *End* and *all nations* go together. Everything God does from now until the end is going to involve nations.

People ask, "Why are you talking about money?" Because it is going to take money to reach the nations. The nations are immersed in darkness, waiting for the light. We can't reach them without money, and we aren't going to be able to reach them if we are broke.

God, however, has money in reserve that has been stored up just for the last days. He isn't hiding the money *from* us; He is hiding it *for* us. It is God's "harvest account," and it is all the money the Church will need to bring in the harvest in these last days. So God is not going to have to hock the pearly gates to be able to finance the harvest of the last days. He is the One who put all the money on this Earth in the first place.

It's in the World System

"Well, where is all of that money?" someone will ask. God has always blessed His people and has met their needs abundantly, just as He said He would. But God has left a majority of the money in His "harvest account" in the hands of the world and allowed them to heap it together for the last days. Why? Because "...the children of this world are in their generation wiser than the children of light" (Luke 16:8). The world's goal is to make money. They spend all their time learning how to make it grow. They have been stockpiling it for generations, drawing interest in money markets, CDs, stocks, and bonds.

Believers, on the other hand, are builders. In whose hands would you leave the money? If God had given the money to the Church, we would have figured a way to spend it all. So God left it in the hands of those who operate in the world system to multiply it until the Church needs it!

But the money was never meant for the devil and his kids. God placed the money here for His children. After the fall of Adam, the money eventually found its way into the hands of the world, and for years the world has been endeavoring to multiply that money. The money has been in the world system — but now it is time for a great transfer of the wealth in the world into the hands of those in the Church who will use it to bring in the end-time harvest.

God is saying, "I have a 'harvest account.' It's out there in the world, and I'm about to call it in!"

Chapter 3
The Great Transfer

Most of us have placed a certain limit on what we think God can do where money is concerned. What we need to realize is that we are in the last days, and restoration is coming to the Church. It is time for the Church to take the limits off God. God will bring the money into our hands in these last days in ways that will amaze us.

Notice throughout the Bible that every time God was ready for a major move, one of the first things He did was transfer an abundance of money to His people. The Bible says in First Corinthians 10:11, "Now all these things happened unto them [Israel] for ensamples [or examples]: and they are written for our admonition, upon whom the ends of the world are come." This passage is talking about us. We are the generation upon whom the ends of the world are come.

We should study the things that happened to Israel and learn from their example. What worked in the "shadow" of the Old Testament will work in the "light," except it will work much better in the light in which we are now living.

God has made numerous financial transfers throughout the history of the world to accomplish His plans. In Exodus 3, when Israel came out of the bondage of Egypt, God moved supernaturally to bring them out with the spoil of the Egyptians:

EXODUS 3:20-22
20 And I will stretch out my hand, and smite Egypt with all my WONDERS which I will do in the midst thereof: and after that he will let you go.

> **21 And I will give this people FAVOUR in the sight
> of the Egyptians: and it shall come to pass, that,
> when ye go, YE SHALL NOT GO EMPTY:**
> **22 But every woman shall borrow of her neigh-
> bour, and of her that sojourneth in her house,
> JEWELS OF SILVER, and JEWELS OF GOLD, and
> RAIMENT: and ye shall put them upon your sons,
> and upon your daughters; and YE SHALL SPOIL
> THE EGYPTIANS.**

God was able to transfer the wealth of Egypt into the
hands of His people through signs, wonders, and favor.
The children of Israel acquired enough wealth to sustain
them in the wilderness for the next 40 years and still
had enough left to build God's tabernacle. Someone will
ask, "Wasn't that stealing for the children of Israel to
take all the wealth of Egypt?"

No, the children of Israel were not stealing from
Egypt. If we go back to the Book of Genesis, we will see
how God used an Israelite named Joseph to bring the
wealth into Egypt in the first place. So it couldn't be
wrong to use 3 million Israelites to take the wealth out of
Egypt. God performed a great transfer to return to the
children of Israel what was rightfully theirs all along.

The Promised Land Account

Joshua 6 gives us another example of a great transfer
of wealth. When the children of Israel left the bondage of
Egypt, God provided them with enough wealth and goods
to sustain them in the wilderness. We could say Israel
gained a "wilderness account" from Egypt. And notice
the first thing God did when the children of Israel
entered the Promised Land. He provided them with a
"Promised Land account."

If we study the scriptures, we will find that when Israel entered the Promised Land, they had to start taking nations. But before they could do that, God instructed them to take the city of Jericho. History tells us the walls around the city of Jericho were so thick, they could run chariot races around the top! Why do you suppose the walls were that thick? Because behind those walls was the wealth necessary to take Israel into the nations God had promised them through His covenant with Abraham.

Taking the Nations

The Promised Land was a land of nations. In that land were the Hivites, the Jebusites, the Canaanites, and all the other "ites" who had to be driven out in order for God's people to possess the land, or "take nations." So God gave Joshua a key or a plan to take the city of Jericho.

The children of Israel were to march around the city for six days without uttering a sound. Then, on the seventh day, they were to march around the city seven times, and on the seventh time around, they were to let out a shout.

> **JOSHUA 6:16**
> **16 And it came to pass at the seventh time, when the priests blew with the trumpets, Joshua said unto the people, SHOUT; FOR THE LORD HATH GIVEN YOU THE CITY.**

What happened?

> **JOSHUA 6:20**
> **20 So the people shouted when the priests blew with the trumpets: and it came to pass, when the**

people heard the sound of the trumpet, and the people shouted with a great shout, that the wall fell down flat, so that the people went up into the city, every man straight before him, and THEY TOOK THE CITY.

The children of Israel utterly destroyed the city of Jericho and took for the treasury of the Lord all the silver, the gold, and vessels of brass and iron (Joshua 6:21,24). Thus, God's "Promised Land account" was transferred into the hands of the children of Israel so they could take the rest of the nations awaiting them in the Promised Land.

Jehoshaphat's Battle Plan

Consider also what happened in Second Chronicles 20. Jehoshaphat was about to go into battle, but he needed a battle plan from God.

2 CHRONICLES 20:18
18 And Jehoshaphat bowed his head with his face to the ground: and all Judah and the inhabitants of Jerusalem fell before the Lord, worshipping the Lord.

When Jehoshaphat and all Judah needed direction from God, they fell on their faces and worshipped Him. They got in the presence of God. Verse 21 shows us the plan God gave to Jehoshaphat:

2 CHRONICLES 20:21
21 And when he had consulted with the people, he appointed SINGERS unto the Lord, and that should praise the beauty of holiness, as THEY WENT OUT BEFORE THE ARMY, and to say, Praise the Lord; for his mercy endureth for ever.

Have you ever noticed God will sometimes give you something to do that doesn't make sense in the natural? God gave Jehoshaphat a plan. He told Jehoshaphat to send the praisers out *ahead* of the army. "And when they began to sing and to praise, the Lord set ambushments against the children of Ammon, Moab, and mount Seir..." (2 Chronicles 20:22). As Jehoshaphat's army approached, they found their enemies already slain — their enemies had destroyed themselves (2 Chronicles 20:23,24)!

As a result, another great transfer took place in verse 25:

> **2 CHRONICLES 20:25**
> **25 And when Jehoshaphat and his people came to TAKE AWAY THE SPOIL of them, they found among them in ABUNDANCE both RICHES with the dead bodies, and PRECIOUS JEWELS, which they stripped off for themselves, more than they could carry away: and they were three days in gathering of the spoil, it was so much.**

How would you like to get so much spoil it takes three days to carry it all away? If it worked in the Old Testament, it will work in the New Testament! God brought finances into the hands of His people then, and He is bringing finances into the hands of the Church to do the work of God in these last days.

Four Lepers and a Move of God

What about the great transfer of wealth we read about in Second Kings 6 and 7? The Syrians had surrounded the city of Samaria and cut off all their supplies. Inside the city, the people were starving to death.

2 KINGS 6:24,25
24 And it came to pass after this, that Benhadad king of Syria gathered all his host, and went up, and besieged Samaria.
25 And there was a great famine in Samaria: and, behold, they besieged it, until an ass's head was sold for fourscore pieces of silver, and the fourth part of a cab of dove's dung for five pieces of silver.

The people were so hungry they were eating ass's head, dove's dung, and verse 29 says they were eating their own children! But the prophet of God said by the Holy Ghost, "...Tomorrow about this time shall a measure of fine flour be sold for a shekel, and two measures of barley for a shekel, in the gate of Samaria" (2 Kings 7:1).

What did God do? He found four lepers who were starving to death outside the city. The lepers began to reason among themselves that if they stayed where they were, they would probably die of starvation. If they went into the city, they would probably die because there was no food there either. If they went to the Syrians, they would probably die because the Syrians would kill them. This didn't leave them with many options. They decided that their best option was to go to the Syrians, because at least they might get something to eat.

Early that morning, the four lepers made their way to the camp of the Syrians. The Syrians couldn't see anyone coming, but they heard what sounded like hundreds of people. They thought the Samaritans had hired other armies to come and do battle. It so frightened the Syrians that they took off running for their lives. What happened? Through one move of God, the Lord supernaturally made four lepers sound like an entire army!

When the four lepers arrived at the Syrian camp, they found it deserted, with an abundant transfer awaiting them.

2 KINGS 7:8
8 And when these lepers came to the uttermost part of the camp, they went into one tent, and did eat and drink, and carried thence SILVER, and GOLD, and RAIMENT, and went and hid it....

The lepers also sent word to Samaria of this good fortune, and the people came and spoiled the tents of the Syrians. The words of the prophet Elisha came to pass just as they were spoken (2 Kings 7:16).

One day four lepers and an entire city were starving to death, and the next day they were stuffing money in their pockets, gathering nice clothes, and eating and drinking until they were satisfied. There was so much wealth in the camp of the Syrians that when it was transferred into the hands of the people of Samaria, it changed the economy of the entire city!

The Cave of Adullam

When God was ready to drive out the Philistines, He chose a shepherd boy named David. Saul was the king at that time, and he had all the money, the armies, the chariots, and the horses. Even though Saul had the equipment, he had lost the anointing of God on his life. So God found David, anointed him as king, and sent him, not to a castle, but to a cave. First Samuel 22 talks about a place called the Cave of Adullam.

1 SAMUEL 22:1
1 David therefore departed thence, and escaped to the cave Adullam: and when his brethren and

all his father's house heard it, they went down thither to him.

David didn't have a 50,000-man army surrounding him. He had 400 men with him in the cave who were in distress, in debt, and discontented (1 Samuel 22:2). But those 400 men became known as "David's mighty men of valor," and together they drove the Philistines out of God's land. In the years to come, as David and his men obeyed God and walked in their covenant, they successfully overcame their enemies without even a wound in battle. So much wealth came into the hands of David and his mighty men of valor that David was able to give more than $1 billion worth of silver, gold, and other valuables out of his own personal account toward the building of Solomon's Temple (2 Chronicles 5). In fact, David and his mighty men combined gave more than $3.42 billion. That's not bad for a team who started out in a cave in distress, in debt, and discontented! They conquered the Philistines, brought peace to the land, and helped build a multi-billion-dollar facility.

Unlikely To Do the Unusual

It's amazing whom God will use to accomplish His plans in the Earth. He chose four lepers, the lowest form of humanity in that day, as a channel to save an entire city. He chose an unlikely shepherd boy, anointed him as king, and used him to lead 400 unlikely men into victory over the Philistine armies and take nations for God. God will use the most unlikely people in the most unusual ways.

I've heard people say, "God couldn't use me."

If God could use four lepers and 400 discouraged men, don't you think He could use you?

"Well, I wasn't born with a lot of money."

You don't have to be.

"But you don't know my family."

You're looking at the wrong family! When you were born again, you were born into God's family!

God isn't looking for our *ability*; He is looking for our *availability*. He is looking for people who will be a channel for His blessings to flow through. In fact, look at Psalm 113:

> **PSALM 113:7,8**
> **7 HE RAISETH UP THE POOR out of the dust, AND LIFTETH THE NEEDY out of the dunghill;**
> **8 That he may SET HIM WITH PRINCES, even with the princes of his people.**

We have often thought that to be poor is to be *spiritual*, but God calls poverty a "dunghill." God's description of poverty in verse 7 is dust and dunghill. God said He will raise the poor out of both the dust and the dunghill and set him with princes. You may not have two nickels to rub together, but if you will make yourself available to God, watch what He will do with you!

We are headed for the greatest transfer of wealth the world has ever seen, and God is looking for people who will say, "I'm just like those 400 men in the Cave of Adullam. I'm in distress, in debt, and discontented. God, use me!"

I remember ministering in a certain church a few years ago. Before the service, the pastor pointed out a man sitting at the back of the sanctuary. He asked me, "Do you see that man?"

"Yes," I said.

The pastor told me when they had first started the church, services were held in a little strip mall. Almost every service, the man the pastor pointed out would stumble across the parking lot, drunk. The man didn't have a dime to his name.

One day he stumbled into the church and sat down. The people welcomed him. That day he gave his life to the Lord. Then he was baptized in the Holy Ghost and started being a doer of the Word of God. After only a few years, that man now owned 13 businesses and was the biggest giver in the church! God raised him out of the dunghill and set him with princes! God is no respecter of persons. He never uses people based on their abilities, but rather on their willingness to be used by Him.

The Wealth of the Wicked

God has transferred the wealth in the world into the hands of His people throughout history. When God brought Israel out of Egypt, He gave us a picture of Israel coming out of the land of *not enough*. Under Pharaoh's command, the Israelites were expected to build cities for the Egyptians using bricks made of mud and straw. They were never given enough materials to make the bricks properly.

Then God took them through the wilderness, or the land of *just enough*. In the wilderness, God supplied them with fresh manna from heaven every day. But the Lord instructed Moses to tell them to go out each morning and gather only enough manna for that day and not to store any for the next day (Exodus 16:16-20). So the Israelites had just enough for each day.

Finally the Lord brought them into the Promised Land, or the land of *more than enough*! The Promised Land is "A land of wheat, and barley, and vines, and fig trees, and pomegranates; a land of oil olive, and honey; A land wherein thou shalt eat bread without scarceness, thou shalt not lack any thing in it; a land whose stones are iron, and out of whose hills thou mayest dig brass" (Deuteronomy 8:8,9). The Israelites had everything they needed in the Promised Land.

We are following in Israel's footsteps. God has promised that money will come into the hands of the Church. Has it happened? It is beginning to happen! Jesus is coming soon. Time is short, so this move will have to happen quickly. What does the Bible say about the money coming into our hands?

PROVERBS 13:22
22 A good man leaveth an inheritance to his children's children: and THE WEALTH OF THE SINNER IS LAID UP FOR THE JUST.

I like the way *The Amplified Bible* translates that verse: "...and the wealth of the sinner [finds its way eventually] into the hands of the righteous, for whom it was laid up." That means the wealth of the sinner will eventually find its way into our hands, because it has been laid up for us! It's not there yet, so it must be on its way!

We don't want to build a doctrine on just one Scripture, so let's look at another, Job 27:13: "This is the portion of a wicked man with God, and the heritage of oppressors,which they shall receive of the Almighty." Verses 16 and 17 show us the portion of the wicked man:

JOB 27:16,17
**16 Though he HEAP UP SILVER as the dust, and
PREPARE RAIMENT as the clay;
17 He may prepare it, but THE JUST SHALL PUT
IT ON, and THE INNOCENT SHALL DIVIDE THE
SILVER.**

In other words, the wicked can store up and stock up
all the wealth they want, but God's people will divide it.
The wicked can prepare their raiment, but the just shall
wear it.

We see this thought again in Proverbs 28:

PROVERBS 28:8
**8   He that by usury and unjust gain increaseth his
substance, he shall gather it for him that will pity
the poor.**

In other words, the wicked will gather and increase,
but the day is coming when he will lose it to those who
pity the poor.

Somebody will say, "Isn't it wrong for God to take
the money out of the hands of the world and give it to
the Church?"

No, it's not. The money was God's in the first place.
Haggai 2:8 says, "The silver is mine, and the gold is
mine, saith the Lord of hosts." As we noted earlier, all
the money belongs to God; it's just out on loan until He
calls it in.

The next verse shows us the same thing:

ECCLESIASTES 2:26
**26 For God giveth to a man that is good in his
sight WISDOM, and KNOWLEDGE, and JOY: but
to the sinner he giveth TRAVAIL, to GATHER and
to HEAP UP, that he may give to him that is good
before God....**

God gives wisdom, knowledge, and joy to those who are good. We, the Church, are in meetings gaining wisdom and knowledge from God's Word. In recent times, God has added an outpouring of joy. So as we are learning, growing, and experiencing a move of the Holy Ghost, the world is laboring, gathering, heaping up, and stockpiling what is needed for the Church to do Her job in the last days. When we see the world prospering, we should not be upset or jealous. Instead, we should shout for joy, because they are gathering it all for us!

Abundance of the Sea

One of the major reasons for God to prosper us is for harvest. We will look at one more portion of Scripture that shows us this in Isaiah 60:

ISAIAH 60:1
1 Arise, shine; for thy light is come, and the glory of the Lord is risen upon thee.

Isaiah is talking about the glory of the Lord coming on God's people.

ISAIAH 60:2
2 For, behold, the darkness shall cover the earth, and gross darkness the people: but the Lord shall arise upon thee, and his glory shall be seen upon thee.

The world is in darkness, and they don't understand the glory, but the Bible says the world is going to be able to *see* something on God's people. What are they going to be able to see? The glory. The glory of God is the power of God, the presence of God, and the joy of the Lord, bringing healing, miracles, favor, and prosperity in every area of our lives.

ISAIAH 60:3
3 And the Gentiles shall come to thy light, and kings to the brightness of thy rising.

Light is development, or we could say increase. When God's people *increase*, the world or the lost are going to come running. And when the world comes running, we have entered the time of harvest!

ISAIAH 60:5
5 Then thou shalt see, and flow together, and thine heart shall fear, and be enlarged; because the ABUNDANCE OF THE SEA shall be converted unto thee, the FORCES of the Gentiles shall come unto thee.

In Scripture, the sea is often a type of a large group of people. Isaiah 60:5 is saying that an abundance of souls will come into the kingdom of God. And when they do, the forces or "wealth," as many translations say, of the world will come in with them!

Transfer for Harvest

A great transfer is coming. The wealth of the world has been laid up for the purpose of bringing in the harvest. The Church has a big job to do in the days, weeks, months, and years ahead. The greatest move of God the world has ever seen is before us. However, for most of us to fulfill what God has for us to do, it will take more money than we've ever seen in our lives. But God is ready to transfer His "harvest account" into the hands of those who know what it's for and what to do with it!

Chapter 4
The Spirit of Prosperity

God wants to do great things in and through the Church. He is looking for people who will think big enough to let Him channel prosperity through them and out to the nations. But have you ever noticed the two areas religion and the devil fight more than anything else? Third John 2 says, "Beloved, I wish [or I pray] above all things that thou mayest prosper and be in health...."

We know John is writing to the Church, because he wouldn't say "beloved" to the world. John said he prayed above everything else that we would prosper and be in health. John knew the importance of these two benefits of redemption. Without them, we would not be so effective in reaching the world for Jesus. But what two areas of doctrine do religion and the devil fight more than any others? Prosperity and health. One thing I never could figure out is why someone would fight for the right to be sick and broke!

John, writing here by the inspiration of the Holy Ghost, says that above everything else he prayed that we would *prosper* and be in health, "...even as thy soul prospereth." The only One who is going to prosper our souls is God. Health and prosperity come out of a relationship with God. They don't replace a relationship with God, but they are directly related to it.

Different Things to Different People

Prosperity means different things to different people. Prosperity is not just a certain dollar amount. If

55

someone has $20 million in the bank but has cancer in his body, prosperity doesn't mean another $1 million; it means healing in his body. If prosperity doesn't touch every area of our lives, it's not prosperity.

Prosperity is not simply money. If it were, we could go to the richest places in the world and find the happiest people, but sometimes the people who have the most money are the most miserable people of all. Prosperity means to go forward, to make progress, or to move ahead. Basically, prosperity means being in and doing the will of God — and it takes money to do the will of God. So money is a *part* of prosperity. But if money is the only part we have, we will be miserable.

Proverbs 10:22 says, "The blessing of the Lord, it maketh rich, and he addeth no sorrow with it." Financial prosperity alone will not do us much good unless it comes from our walk with God.

God wants us to have a *lifestyle* of prosperity that touches every area of our lives. It's like throwing a rock into a pond — the ripples go out and touch every shore. If we get into God's system of prosperity, it won't just touch our wallets or our bank account; it will touch our home, family, and church, and go out in every direction.

We know a man in Kenya whose ministry reaches several countries in the eastern region of Africa. During one visit, he took us out to the bush country to show us his house. It was a two-story house with a brand-new tin roof. He told us, "I'm a prosperous man in the bush country of Kenya. This might not be prosperity where you live, but where I live, this is considered prosperity."

This man taught prosperity to his people. He said, "If we don't teach them prosperity, they won't have prosperity."

He told us, "I teach my people to believe God, and before long they are riding bicycles instead of walking. Then, if they stay with it, they get motorcycles. As they keep believing God, some have cars given to them. One man even had a full-size bus given to him!"

Not Just an American Gospel

If the nations are to prosper, those who are called to go to the nations will have to preach *all* of the Gospel. Many American missionaries have not taught that prosperity belongs to everyone, and in doing so, they have robbed the nations. We have actually tried to *be* God to the nations, but America is not the pot of gold at the end of the rainbow.

I was talking once with a man I hadn't seen in years. The last time I saw him, I had just graduated from Bible school, and he was not yet saved. A few years later, he was born again and became a pastor. By the time our paths crossed again, more years had passed. We began to talk, and within a few minutes he said, "I don't believe like you do."

I said, "Oh, you don't? How do you know?"

"First," he said, "you believe God wants everyone healed."

"I am guilty as charged. I believe it is God's highest and best to have everyone healed. I believe God wants people healed as much as He wants them saved."

Then the man said, "You believe in that prosperity stuff, too, don't you?"

"Guilty again!"

"Well, I don't believe in it," he said. "That is just *an American Gospel*."

There is no such thing as an *American* Gospel. Jesus Himself said, "...Go ye into all the world, and preach the gospel to every creature" (Mark 16:15). If the Gospel doesn't work equally for every individual, it is not *the* Gospel.

I told the man, "You have gotten to me too late, brother. I have been to Africa. I have been to Australia. I have been to Central America. I have been to India. And do you know what I found? The only reason the Gospel doesn't work is because some people don't have the nerve to preach it!"

If we don't preach the New Birth, people will not be born again. If we don't preach healing, people will not be healed. If we don't preach prosperity, people will not prosper.

The Gospel we preach is not an American Gospel. The problem is that America tried to keep it to herself for a long time, but if we will preach the full Gospel, it will work anywhere!

Jesus said, "And this gospel of the kingdom shall be preached in all the world for a witness unto all nations; and then shall the end come" (Matthew 24:14). A key to the end coming is *this* Gospel being preached to the nations. Some might say, "We don't believe in prosperity; we just preach the Gospel." What Gospel was Jesus referring to in Luke 4:18? "The Spirit of the Lord is upon me, because he hath anointed me to preach the gospel to the poor...." Jesus preached the Good News to the *poor*. The only good news to the poor would be, "You don't have to be poor anymore!"

Prosperity may mean different things to different people in different situations, but the bottom line is: God wants us to prosper wherever we are located.

A Revelation of Prosperity

I've heard people say, "Healing was easy for me to receive, but prosperity sure was difficult." For me it was the opposite. When I was first saved, I didn't need healing in my body; I needed prosperity. I was working in the real estate business, which is the kind of business that if you don't sell, you don't eat. I didn't sell anything for months, so that ought to tell you something! The first thing I needed was a revelation of prosperity.

I tried everything I knew to do to make it work. I begged, pleaded, bawled, and squalled. I even fasted. I went to meetings and tried to get someone to prophesy prosperity over me. I didn't understand that prosperity had already been bought and paid for with the precious blood of Jesus. I didn't know prosperity already belonged to me.

After a number of months, I finally gave up trying to do it myself. I went to my office and closed the door. I told the secretary to hold all my calls (which was a faith statement itself). I closed my eyes and let my Bible fall open. That is not being led by the Holy Ghost, but sometimes God will work with us when we don't know any better. Later on, I thought, *Thank God it didn't fall open to the Book of Leviticus and all the animal sacrifices!* Thank God, it fell open to the New Testament Book of Philippians.

My God Shall Supply All My Need

I started reading in Philippians. I read chapters 1 through 3. Then I got to Philippians 4:19, which says, "But my God shall supply all your need according to his riches in glory by Christ Jesus."

I read it a second time. Then I heard myself say out loud, "I wish I could believe that."

After reading it a few more times, I had it memorized. But just because we have something memorized does not mean we believe it. We can have a thousand scriptures in our head, but when we get one in our heart, it will change our lives forever! I figured if it took one scripture to get me saved and one scripture to get me baptized with the Holy Ghost, if I could get one scripture in my heart on prosperity, I would be prosperous.

After a few weeks of reading and thinking on that verse, it suddenly seemed to drop down on the inside of me. Luke 9:44 says, "Let these sayings sink down into your ears...."

It didn't happen overnight, but as I stayed with the Word, it got inside and stayed with me. It got "down into my ears."

The next time someone asked me if I was making any money, as I tried to answer, I found myself saying, "My God supplies all my need." It wasn't intentional. I just could not seem to talk poverty or lack anymore. Jesus said in Matthew 12:34, "...out of the abundance of the heart the mouth speaketh." If we don't "talk" poverty, we won't "walk" it!

When Philippians 4:19 got down on the inside of me in 1974, I didn't instantly have more money in my pocket. But from that time until now, God has been my Source. I don't need to figure out how to get people to give money to me or how to have my needs met. My God supplies all my need, and I let Him choose the channels He wants to use to bring it to me.

Prosperity Is a Grace

We noted earlier that Jesus became poor for our sakes that through His poverty we might be rich (2 Corinthians 8:9). Along those same lines, let's look at Second Corinthians 9:

> **2 CORINTHIANS 9:8**
> **8 And God is able to make all GRACE abound toward you; that ye, ALWAYS HAVING ALL SUFFICIENCY in all things, may abound to every good work.**

Paul called prosperity a grace. Notice it is never called a *curse*. Paul also said "...God is *able* to make all grace abound toward you...." He didn't say it would happen automatically. He said God is *able*. In the same way, God is able and willing for all to be saved, but we still have to do something to receive salvation.

People say, "Well, if God wants me to prosper, He'll just do it." That is like saying, "If God wants me to get saved, He'll do it." A person could die and go to hell thinking that way! No, we have to do something to walk in the blessings of God.

Abundance Mentality

One way of walking in the blessings of God as far as prosperity is concerned is to start thinking more like God thinks. Writing to the Corinthians, Paul said, "We having the same spirit of faith, according as it is written, I believed, and therefore have I spoken; we also believe, and therefore speak" (2 Corinthians 4:13). Did you notice Paul didn't say, "We having the same *principles* of faith," or "the same *doctrine* of faith"? Don't misunderstand me — the teaching of faith is absolutely necessary, but as someone has said, "The principles of faith can be *taught*, but the spirit of faith has to be *caught*."

It is no different in the area of prosperity. It's one thing to know the principles of prosperity and to place them in neat, perfect order. However, that does not mean we are walking in prosperity. We need to catch a *spirit* of prosperity.

Someone will ask, "Is there another spirit besides the Holy Spirit?" No. What we mean is an *attitude*. It's about time the Church developed an attitude where prosperity is concerned. A spirit or an attitude of prosperity will cause us to think bigger. It will take our blinders off, lengthen our cords, strengthen our stakes, and gird up the loins of our minds.

In essence, a spirit of prosperity will cause us to think more like God thinks. God thinks big. For example, if someone says the word "water," we probably think of a glass of water. But when God hears the word "water," He thinks of all the lakes, rivers, streams, and oceans on Earth. What happens when we hear the word "wood"? We may think of a table. But when God hears the word "wood," He thinks of all the trees in all the forests in the world. It's time we started thinking like God thinks!

The Church has been poverty-minded. Before I came into God's plan for my life, I had a few plans of my own, but being sick, poor, and sorry weren't any of them! That's not to say that we in the Church should be money-minded. Money can be neither our motivation nor our highest priority. What we must realize is that the Church needs to move out of a *lack* mentality and into an *abundance* mentality. We're going to have to do things God's way if we want the world to get involved. That doesn't mean we should be extravagant; it just means we should do things right. It means we in the Church should get our thinking straightened out and dig ourselves out of some of the ruts we've been in where prosperity is concerned.

I've heard people say, "You don't understand; I'm on a limited income."

The only thing that limits our income is us! It's about time we started thinking like God thinks. He said in Isaiah 55:8,9, "For my thoughts are not your thoughts, neither are your ways my ways, saith the Lord. For as the heavens are higher than the earth, so are my ways higher than your ways, and my thoughts than your thoughts." It's time to move from a poverty mentality to an abundance mentality, because important things need to be accomplished for the kingdom of God, and they need to be done in grand and glorious style!

God's Definition of Prosperity

God wants us to *abound* to every good work not barely get by. God's definition of prosperity is *an abundant supply*. The *Amplified* translation of Second Corinthians 9:8 says, "And God is able to make all grace (every favor and earthly blessing) come to you in abundance, so that you may always and under all circumstances and whatever the need, be self-sufficient — possessing enough to require no aid or support and furnished in abundance for every good work and charitable donation." God's definition of prosperity is abundance for us with plenty left over to give to every good work.

Prosperity is not provided just so we will have abundance for ourselves. Paul said in Philippians 4:17, "Not because I desire a gift: but I desire fruit that may abound to your account." Have you ever noticed fruit has two parts? Fruit has something to *eat* and something to *plant*. So Paul is saying we have something to benefit us and something to sow into every good work.

What happens when we plant our seed? It multiplies! That means we have more to eat and more to sow. God doesn't operate on the principles of subtraction or addition; He operates on the principles of multiplication. We need to understand that God wants to bless us not so we can see how much we can *get*, but so we can see how much we can *give*.

Power To Get Wealth

God told His people in Deuteronomy 8:

DEUTERONOMY 8:18
18 But thou shalt remember the Lord thy God: for it is he that giveth thee POWER to get WEALTH....

Prosperity is God's idea! It is God who gives us the ability to get wealth. I looked up that word "power" and found it is also translated "substance" or "wealth." If we read Deuteronomy 8:18 with that in mind, it says, "it is he that giveth thee *wealth* to get *wealth*."

In other words, God gives us wealth — or something to sow — in order for us to gain more wealth. God gives us the seed to plant that will cause fruit to abound to our account (Philippians 4:17).

What else does Deuteronomy 8:18 say?

18 ...that he may ESTABLISH HIS COVENANT which he sware unto thy fathers, as it is this day.

This verse has a twofold meaning. First, God gives us power to get wealth so He can establish His covenant *to* us. Prosperity is a major part of God's covenant with man. Without the blessing of prosperity, God's covenant is not fully established in our lives.

Second, God gives us the power to get wealth so He can establish His covenant *through* us, which will enable us to take the Gospel to the world. When God prospers us, He is establishing His covenant. So for God to fully establish His covenant to us, He prospers us.

Psalm 35:27 says, "Let them shout for joy, and be glad, that favour my righteous cause...." What is God's righteous cause? The world, the nations, and the heathen — the lost! God said, "Ask of me, and I shall give thee the heathen for thine inheritance, and the uttermost parts of the earth for thy possession" (Psalm 2:8).

The last half of Psalm 35:27 says, "...yea, let them say continually, Let the Lord be magnified, which hath pleasure in the prosperity of his servant." God takes *pleasure* in our prosperity! Aren't we considered His servants? Notice in verse 27, the word "servant" is singular. God wants to touch individuals with the blessings of prosperity. It's just like a hose — water may flow out the end of the hose to water something, but the hose gets wet in the process. When God uses us as a channel of blessing, we are blessed, too!

A spirit of prosperity is coming on the Church in these last days. God is endeavoring to transfer great prosperity to the Church so we can afford to bring in the harvest for which He is waiting. If God can get prosperity *through* us, He will get it *to* us!

Chapter 5
Covenant Blessings

God has set forth promises in His Word concerning prosperity, but if we don't know what those promises are, we will not take advantage of what God has provided for us. Most of us have thought that to be poor means to be humble. In fact, I thought to serve God and be in the ministry, I had to be broke. The first time I saw a preacher driving a nice automobile, I thought, *Isn't that nice? Some businessman must have loaned that preacher a car so he could drive to church.*

But no matter what our opinions or what we have been taught, the basis of truth is always the Word of God. So we want to look at the scriptures and find just what God has provided for us and what belongs to us where prosperity is concerned.

Redeemed From the Curse

Galatians 3:13 tells us we have been redeemed from the curse of the law:

GALATIANS 3:13
13 Christ HATH REDEEMED US from the CURSE OF THE LAW, being made a curse for us: for it is written, Cursed is every one that hangeth on a tree.

The Bible said Christ redeemed us. According to *W. E. Vine's Expository Dictionary*, to redeem means "to buy, to purchase, or to release on receipt of ransom." Years ago in America, we had a widespread system called S & H Green Stamps. With this system, every time you purchased food at the grocery store, gasoline at the gas station, or items at department stores, you were given green-colored stamps to paste into booklets.

Once all the pages were filled with stamps, the booklet could be taken to what was called a Redemption Center. There was a catalog showing all the items available at the Redemption Center, including camping supplies, gifts, toys, linens, and all kinds of items for the kitchen. The catalog showed all the merchandise, but no prices were listed. Instead, it said, "5 books of Green Stamps," or "25 books of Green Stamps necessary to purchase item."

Once I found a sleeping bag for camping, and I wanted it so badly. It took quite a few booklets of Green Stamps to buy the sleeping bag, so I saved and saved until I had enough booklets. I could have had all the money in the world, but I still would not have been able to buy one thing out of that catalog. The Redemption Center didn't take money; it took Green Stamps. You had to take your booklets full of Green Stamps to the Redemption Center and then you could redeem your prize.

Man fell into sin in the Garden of Eden, and that sin had a price. There was only one way to purchase man from sin. Man couldn't buy his way out of it. He couldn't get out by doing good works. Sin demanded a different price — a greater price than money. Sin demanded a sinless, spotless Sacrifice who came in the form of a man. That man is Jesus. Jesus came to Earth, went to the cross, and shed His blood. Through His death, burial, and resurrection, He paid the price and redeemed His prize. All the money in the world could not have bought us. But Jesus redeemed or bought us back with His own precious blood.

Galatians 3:13 says, "Christ *hath* redeemed us...."
When Jesus died on the cross, He said, "...It is finished..."
(John 19:30). The price of sin had been paid. Jesus
purchased our redemption and then went to the Father's
right hand to enforce His New Covenant.

We have been redeemed from the curse of the broken
law. What is the curse of the law? First, the curse
contained spiritual death or separation from God
(Genesis 2:17). Deuteronomy 28 shows us all the
blessings of keeping the law as well as more of the curse
of breaking the law.

In verses 15 through 61, we see the curse contained
every sickness and disease known to mankind. And it
also contained poverty. Galatians 3:13 says we are
redeemed from all those curses. We are redeemed from
spiritual death. We are redeemed from sickness and
disease. And we are redeemed from poverty.

It is one thing to know what we have been redeemed
from, but verse 14 tells us what we are redeemed *to*.

GALATIANS 3:13,14
**13 Christ hath redeemed us from the curse of the
law, being made a curse for us: for it is written,
Cursed is every one that hangeth on a tree:
14 That the BLESSING OF ABRAHAM might come
on the Gentiles through Jesus Christ; that we might
receive the promise of the Spirit through faith.**

What is the blessing of Abraham? Let's go to
Genesis 12 and find out.

Blessed To Be a Blessing

GENESIS 12:1-3
**1   Now the Lord had said unto Abram, Get thee out
of thy country, and from thy kindred, and from thy
father's house, unto a land that I will shew thee:**

> **2   And I will make of thee a great nation, and I will BLESS THEE, and make thy name great; and THOU SHALT BE A BLESSING:**
> **3   And I will bless them that bless thee, and curse him that curseth thee: and IN THEE SHALL ALL FAMILIES OF THE EARTH BE BLESSED.**

God told Abram, "...I will bless thee, and make thy name great; and thou shalt be a blessing" (Genesis 12:2). God has a twofold purpose in mind with prosperity: first is to bless us and second is to make us a blessing. This is the very basis of prosperity. We can't be a blessing until we're blessed. At the Gate Beautiful, Peter said, "...such as I have give I thee..." (Acts 3:6). We can't give what we don't have.

Why does God want to prosper His people? Because He loves us! It gives Him great pleasure to bless us, not just for us, but also so that we can be a blessing to the world. As we noted previously, Psalm 35:27 tells us, "Let them shout for joy, and be glad, that favour my righteous cause: yea, let them say continually, Let the Lord be magnified, which hath pleasure in the prosperity of his servant." God takes pleasure in our prosperity! God also said in Genesis 12:3, "And I will bless them that bless thee, and curse him that curseth thee: and in thee shall all families of the earth be blessed."

Abraham's Blessings

We are a part of Abraham's family, and we should be blessed like faithful Abraham. Just how blessed was Abraham?

> **GENESIS 13:2**
> **2   And Abram was VERY RICH in cattle, in silver, and in gold.**

Abram, whose name God changed to Abraham, was rich in anything that could be used as currency. When Abram left his country, he took his wife, Sarai, and his nephew, Lot. As Abram stepped out to obey God and walked in his covenant, he and Lot were so blessed the land couldn't contain them both.

> **GENESIS 13:5,6**
> **5 And Lot also, which went with Abram, had flocks, and herds, and tents.**
> **6 And the land was not able to bear them, that they might dwell together: for their SUBSTANCE WAS GREAT, so that they could not dwell together.**

Abraham's covenant with God was so strong that Lot also became very rich. Lot didn't have the covenant, but he was in partnership with a man who did.

Covenant vs. Contract

Notice God didn't make a contract with Abraham; He made a covenant. A contract is for a time span and for a particular transfer or transaction. A covenant is for eternity, and it includes *every part* of life. As long as one of the persons involved in the making of that covenant is alive, he is committed to enforce the covenant to an heir of the person on the other side.

Abraham may have died, but God will never die. Therefore, He looks for a descendant on Abraham's side of that covenant to whom He can give the blessings. In other words, by covenant we mean, "What is yours is mine and what is mine is yours. If you die, I'll look for the closest one to you so I can give him or her the same blessings. Then, if that person dies, I'll look for the next in line. As long as I am alive, that covenant is in effect, and I will be looking for someone on whom to pour the blessings."

David and Jonathan

A prime example of this can be found in the covenant between David and Jonathan in the Book of First Samuel. After David had killed Goliath (1 Samuel 17), he met Saul's son, Jonathan. The Bible says in First Samuel 18 that David and Jonathan had a bond between them.

> **1 SAMUEL 18:1,3**
> **1   And it came to pass, when he had made an end of speaking unto Saul, that the soul of Jonathan was knit with the soul of David, and Jonathan loved him as his own soul...**
> **3   Then Jonathan and David made a COVENANT, because he loved him as his own soul.**

The minute David and Jonathan made a covenant, Jonathan took his sword, his armor, and everything he had and gave it to David. Later, both Saul and Jonathan were killed in battle. David's covenant partner was gone, but the covenant was still alive. So if Jonathan had any descendants, it was up to David to find them and pour the blessings of the covenant on them. Second Samuel 9:1 says, "And David said, Is there yet any that is left of the house of Saul, that I may shew him kindness for Jonathan's sake?"

It just so happened that Jonathan had a son named Mephibosheth, who was lame. He lived in the poorest section of town; he didn't have good health; and he didn't have any wealth. But there was one thing he did have — he was a descendant of one who had a covenant with the man who became king.

When David was made aware of Jonathan's heir, he sent for Mephibosheth. David told him, "You are going to sit at my table and eat of my food. You are going to have access to my servants, and you are going to live in my house. Everything I have belongs to you because I had a covenant with your father."

If we follow the scriptures, we will see this same system in God's covenant with Abraham. Every time we find one of Abraham's descendants, we find Abraham's blessings. We've seen that Abraham was blessed. And when Abraham died, his blessing, by covenant, passed to his heir.

Isaac's Blessings

When Abraham died, God looked for the next in line — Abraham's promised son, Isaac. God spoke to Isaac in Genesis 26, saying:

GENESIS 26:3-5
3 Sojourn in this land, and I will be with thee, and will bless thee; for unto thee, and unto thy seed, I will give all these countries, and I WILL PERFORM THE OATH WHICH I SWARE UNTO ABRAHAM THY FATHER;
4 And I will make thy seed to multiply as the stars of heaven, and will give unto thy seed all these countries; and IN THY SEED SHALL ALL THE NATIONS OF THE EARTH BE BLESSED;
5 Because that Abraham obeyed my voice, and kept my charge, my commandments, my statutes, and my laws.

In other words, Abraham obeyed God, and Isaac was Abraham's descendant. What God gave to Abraham, He also gave to Isaac.

At that time there was a great famine in the land. But in verse 12, God showed Isaac the covenant he had was greater than the famine.

> **GENESIS 26:12-14**
> **12 Then Isaac sowed in that land, and received in the same year an hundredfold: and THE LORD BLESSED HIM.**
> **13 And the man waxed great, and went forward, and grew until he BECAME VERY GREAT:**
> **14 For he had possession of flocks, and possession of herds, and great store of servants: and the Philistines envied him.**

The Philistines were the "heathen" or the "world." Isaac was so blessed, the world envied him! Remember, this was in the middle of a famine. Why did these blessings come on Isaac? Because he stepped into Abraham's covenant.

What about Isaac's son, Jacob — the next heir after Isaac?

Jacob's Blessings

> **GENESIS 28:20-22**
> **20 And Jacob vowed a vow, saying, If God will be with me, and will keep me in this way that I go, and will give me bread to eat, and raiment to put on,**
> **21 So that I come again to my father's house in peace; then shall the Lord be my God:**
> **22 And this stone, which I have set for a pillar, shall be God's house: and of all that thou shalt give me I will surely give the tenth unto thee.**

Jacob knew the beginning of God's blessings started with the tithe. Look at the result in Genesis 30:43, "And the man increased *exceedingly*, and had much cattle, and maidservants, and menservants, and camels, and asses."

Why did all these blessings come to Jacob? Because he stepped into Abraham's covenant! And when Jacob died, his blessings passed by covenant to his son, Joseph.

Joseph's Blessings

Joseph was the man whose brothers sold him into slavery. Naturally speaking, there was no way a slave was going to prosper. *But Joseph had Abraham's covenant.*

Watch what happened to Joseph in Genesis 39 because of Abraham's covenant.

> **GENESIS 39:1,2**
> **1 And Joseph was brought down to Egypt; and Potiphar, an officer of Pharaoh, captain of the guard, an Egyptian, bought him of the hands of the Ishmeelites, which had brought him down thither.**
> **2 AND THE LORD WAS WITH JOSEPH, and he was a PROSPEROUS MAN; and he was in the house of his master the Egyptian.**

God prospered Joseph even while he was a slave in the house of his master! Genesis 39:3 says, "And his master saw that the Lord was with him, and that the Lord made all that he did to prosper in his hand."

As we follow Joseph's life, we see that someone falsely accused him, and he went to prison. It looked as if he was going to spend the rest of his life there. It couldn't have looked any worse. *But Joseph still had his covenant.* He knew something had to change because he had a covenant — an agreement with God made with his forefather. The blessings of Abraham belonged to Joseph, too!

While Joseph was in prison, Pharaoh had a dream. No one could interpret it, and the covenant went into effect — God gave the interpretation to Joseph. In Genesis 41:25-36, Joseph gave the interpretation to Pharaoh's dream, saying there would be seven years of plenty throughout Egypt, followed by seven years of famine. Joseph then proposed that a wise man be set over all of Egypt to store up food in the land against the seven years of famine. Genesis 41:38 says, "And Pharaoh said unto his servants, Can we find such a one as this is, a man in whom the Spirit of God is?"

> **GENESIS 41:39-43**
> **39 And Pharaoh said unto Joseph, Forasmuch as God hath shewed thee all this, there is none so discreet and wise as thou art:**
> **40 Thou shalt be over my house, and according unto thy word shall all my people be ruled: only in the throne will I be greater than thou.**
> **41 And Pharaoh said unto Joseph, See, I have set thee over all the land of Egypt.**
> **42 And Pharaoh took off his ring from his hand, and put it upon Joseph's hand, and arrayed him in vestures of fine linen, and put a gold chain about his neck;**
> **43 And he made him to ride in the second chariot which he had; and they cried before him, Bow the knee: and he made him ruler over all the land of Egypt.**

Pharaoh appointed Joseph to rule over his house. Joseph went from prison to second in command to the ruler of the nation!

Genesis 41:54 says, "And the seven years of dearth began to come, according as Joseph had said: and the dearth was in all lands; but in all the land of Egypt there was bread." God blessed a whole nation because of one man with a covenant. Why? Because the people were so good? No. Because Pharaoh gave authority to a man with a covenant. But the blessing didn't end there.

GENESIS 41:56,57
56 And the famine was over all the face of the earth: And Joseph opened all the storehouses, and sold unto the Egyptians; and the famine waxed sore in the land of Egypt.
57 And all countries came into Egypt to Joseph for to buy corn; because that the famine was so sore in all lands.

Not only did one man supply food for the world, but look at all the wealth he brought into the nation of Egypt. He went from being a slave to being a prisoner to being the ruler of the nation. Why? Because he had a covenant. He was heir to the covenant God gave to Abraham!

David's Blessings

If we continue to follow the covenant, we come to David. David started out as a shepherd boy whom God anointed to be king. In First Samuel 22, David gathered his troops together at a place called the Cave of Adullam. He had 400 men who were in distress, in debt, and discontented — *but they joined a man with a covenant.*

David and his troops didn't have anything materially speaking. King Saul had horses, chariots, troops, money, and the kingdom. But David had the covenant — and the blessings always follow the covenant.

So with 400 men and his covenant, David drove the Philistines out of the land. By the time David's son, Solomon, prepared to build the Temple in First Chronicles 29, David had given more than $1 billion worth of gold out of his own treasury. The man started out in a cave with 400 men who were all in debt, and prospered in his lifetime to the point that he gave, according to today's standards, approximately

$1.4 billion worth of gold to help build the Temple (1 Chronicles 29:3,4).

Further on in Second Chronicles, we find the next generation. God spoke to David's son, Solomon, and said, "Wisdom and knowledge is granted unto thee; and I will give thee riches, and wealth, and honour, such as none of the kings have had that have been before thee, neither shall there any after thee have the like" (2 Chronicles 1:12).

David gave over $1 billion worth of gold, and God told David's son, "I am going to bless you beyond any king that has been before or after you." Solomon was even more prosperous than his father, David. The blessings of the covenant were passed on to Solomon, too.

Promise to One Seed

When Jesus came to Earth, He operated in this same covenant. Galatians 3:16 says, "Now to Abraham and his seed were the promises made. He saith not, And to seeds, as of many; but as of one, And to thy seed, which is Christ." The promise included Abraham and all his descendants — and his seed, Jesus. But the covenant didn't stop with Jesus! The Bible says, "And if ye be Christ's, then are ye Abraham's seed, and heirs according to the promise" (Galatians 3:29). *Those who are born again are heirs to all the blessings of the Abrahamic covenant!*

We didn't get into this covenant by natural progression; we got into this covenant through faith in Jesus Christ. When we were born again, we became Abraham's seed! That means we inherited the same promise. What belonged to Abraham was passed down to Isaac, Jacob, Joseph, David, Solomon, and finally to

Jesus; then we entered the covenant through Jesus. That means what Jesus gets, we get! We are heirs of God and joint heirs with Jesus Christ, according to Romans 8:17.

When people in the Church say, "We don't believe in prosperity," we can tell them, "You can believe anything you want; but we have a covenant."

The wealth in the world is coming our way because we have a covenant. The only way for prosperity to *not* belong to the Church today would be for God to break His covenant with Abraham. God never has done that, and He never will. God is looking for a people who will be bold enough to take off their religious-colored glasses, forget what has been taught for generations, forget what everyone else thinks, and take Him at His word.

Prosperity is part of our covenant blessing. It was bought and paid for by the blood of the Lord Jesus. It rightfully belongs to every born-again believer as part of our inheritance.

The covenant blessings don't come to us because we are such good people, or because God decided He wanted to be nice to us. The blessings come to us because we are in the family of God. The covenant God made with Abraham is still in effect today. It is ours by inheritance, and it encompasses every area of our lives!

Chapter 6
God's System for Increase

In September 1995, I spent extra time in prayer. One thing the Spirit of God spoke to my heart was, "Between now and the end of 1995, a *great surge* will come." A surge is power that shoots through the wires and gets stronger — just like we might see in a storm. However, this storm is a constructive storm, not a destructive one. It's a Holy Ghost storm with the wind of God, the rain of the Holy Ghost, and the lightning of the Spirit of God.

Another thing the Spirit of God said at that time was, "The year 1996 will be a year of *great increase.*" I didn't know if He meant for us individually as a ministry, or for the Body of Christ as a whole. I soon learned that He meant 1996 would be a year of great increase for the entire Church. I watched, and that is exactly what happened for a lot of people in 1996.

Between September and December 1995, our ministry began to experience a great surge. Then, when we stepped into 1996, things began to escalate. There was a momentum we could tangibly feel. We experienced an increase in anointing, in the flow of the Holy Ghost, and in souls — and a strong increase in finances. Increase doesn't mean we ascend for a while and then reach a plateau and level out; increase means God plans for us to keep going higher and higher.

God has a system for increase. If we want God's results, we need to learn God's system. God's system doesn't relate to the natural mind, which is the world's way of thinking. The world's system is to dig, claw, scratch, bite, chew, and run over anybody who is in your way, just to make it to the top and get all you can for yourself.

On the other hand, God's system says, "I am going to bypass the world system of increase, and I am going to prosper you through *farming*."

God: The Original Farmer

Notice how the Bible refers to God in James 5:7: "...Behold, the husbandman...." "Behold" means to keep your eyes on or to watch. Watch the husbandman. Some Bible translations refer to the husbandman as the landman. Others say farmer.

What does a farmer do? He plants the best seed in the best ground he can find. Jesus said in John 12:24, "...Except a corn of wheat fall into the ground and die, it abideth alone: but if it die, it bringeth forth much fruit." Here Jesus called Himself a seed. God wanted a family, so He sowed the best seed this Earth has ever seen — the Lord Jesus Christ — that He might receive many sons unto glory (Hebrews 2:10).

God is the original farmer, and everything in His system works by sowing and reaping. God sowed a seed, and then He reaped a harvest. It's really simple. If we can understand this principle in the natural, we can understand that it pertains to spiritual things as well. If God wants a harvest, He sows a seed. If we want a harvest, we sow a seed.

Increase in God's kingdom always comes by the spiritual law of sowing and reaping, as in Genesis 8:22: "While the earth remaineth, *seedtime* and *harvest*, and cold and heat, and summer and winter, and day and night shall not cease." In First Corinthians 3:6, Paul said, "I have *planted*, Apollos *watered*; but God gave the *increase.*" Notice in both references that increase began with planting.

Sowing and Reaping

The entire kingdom of God operates on the basic principle of sowing and reaping: "Be not deceived; God is not mocked: for whatsoever a man soweth, that shall he also reap" (Galatians 6:7).

Jesus taught His disciples the parable of "The Sower and the Seed" in Mark 4:

> **MARK 4:3-8**
> 3 Hearken; Behold, there went out a sower to sow:
> 4 And it came to pass, as he sowed, some fell by the way side, and the fowls of the air came and devoured it up.
> 5 And some fell on stony ground, where it had not much earth; and immediately it sprang up, because it had no depth of earth:
> 6 But when the sun was up, it was scorched; and because it had no root, it withered away.
> 7 And some fell among thorns, and the thorns grew up, and choked it, and it yielded no fruit.
> 8 And other fell on good ground, and did yield fruit that sprang up and INCREASED; and brought forth, some thirty, and some sixty, and some an hundred.

Jesus described four kinds of ground in which the sower sowed his seed, but Jesus' disciples didn't understand and asked Him to explain this parable.

> **MARK 4:10,11;13**
> 10 And when he was alone, they that were about him with the twelve asked of him the parable.
> 11 And he said unto them, Unto you it is given to know THE MYSTERY OF THE KINGDOM OF GOD:

**but unto them that are without, all these things
are done in parables...
13 And he said unto them, Know ye not this
parable? and how then will ye know all parables?**

In other words, Jesus was saying if the disciples
could not understand sowing and reaping, they would
not understand anything else, because the whole
kingdom of God operates on the law of sowing and
reaping. But we could "flip that coin over" and say, "If
you *do* understand this parable or principle, you will be
able to understand all the rest."

The mystery of the kingdom is simply this: If the
Word is sown in good ground, there will be fruit.

Then Jesus went on to further explain how the
kingdom of God operates:

**MARK 4:26-32
26 And he said, SO IS THE KINGDOM OF GOD, AS
IF A MAN SHOULD CAST SEED INTO THE
GROUND;
27 And should sleep, and rise night and day, and
the seed should spring and grow up, he knoweth
not how.
28 For the earth bringeth forth fruit of herself;
first the blade, then the ear, after that the full corn
in the ear.
29 But when the fruit is brought forth, immediately
he putteth in the sickle, because the harvest is
come.
30 And he said, Whereunto shall we liken the
kingdom of God? or with what comparison shall we
compare it?
31 It is like a grain of mustard SEED, which, when
it is SOWN in the earth, is less than all the seeds
that be in the earth:
32 But WHEN IT IS SOWN, IT GROWETH UP, and
becometh greater than all herbs, and shooteth out**

**great branches; so that the fowls of the air may
lodge under the shadow of it.**

Repeatedly, Jesus is letting us know that the kingdom
of God works according to a law. If we want a harvest or
an increase in any area — sow seed.

Jesus shared another parable in the Book of Matthew:

MATTHEW 13:31,32
**31 Another parable put he forth unto them, saying,
The kingdom of heaven is like to a grain of mustard
seed, which a man took, and SOWED in his field:
32 Which indeed is the least of all seeds: but WHEN
IT IS GROWN, it is THE GREATEST AMONG
HERBS, and becometh a tree, so that the birds of
the air come and lodge in the branches thereof.**

The Spirit of God spoke to me about this verse once,
saying, "The reason a lot of 'birds' don't have 'branches'
to live in is because you keep eating all your seed
instead of planting some and letting it grow."

God Gives Seed to the Sower

God never designed for us to "eat" all of our seed.
What would happen if a farmer purchased all his seed,
brought it home, and said, "This would make good
bread. Let's grind it up and start baking"? It may make
wonderful bread, but if the farmer eats all his seed,
what is he going to harvest next year?

When God puts seed into our hands, we've often
made the mistake of eating our seed instead of sowing
it. The Bible doesn't say that God gives seed to the
eater; it says He gives seed to the *sower*.

When God gives us seed, we are supposed to do
something with it. We are supposed to sow it! Every time

a seed is sown, we can expect a harvest to come up, which means fruit abounding to our account. Fruit always has two parts: something to eat and something to plant. The Bible says that God gives "...seed to the sower, and bread to the eater" (Isaiah 55:10). The more seed we have, the more we will have to sow, and the more bread we will have to eat, and so on until it becomes a lifestyle. When finances come into our hands, we know enough to sow 10 percent into our local church. But we need to check with God concerning the remaining 90 percent to see what part is "feed" and what part is "seed."

Cast Your Bread Upon the Water

The Israelites learned to develop a lifestyle of sowing and reaping. We can see an example of it in the Book of Ecclesiastes:

> **ECCLESIASTES 11:1**
> **1 Cast thy BREAD upon the waters: for thou shalt find it after many days.**

This verse pertains to a time when Israel was a nomadic tribe, which means they spent a lot of time moving from one place to another. Normally, they would follow or stay close to a river as they traveled. So they would gather their seed, eat part, save part to sustain them during travel, and then throw the rest out on the water.

Someone will ask, "Why would they do that? It's a waste to throw good seed in the water when they could be eating it."

What we have to understand is that they had just gathered their seed at harvest time. Harvest time was when latter rains fell and caused the river to overflow its banks. As they cast their seed upon the water, the water carried the seed downstream. And when the rains stopped, the rivers receded and left the seed on the banks, where all the rich soil was deposited. By the time the Israelites arrived where the seed was planted, there was a harvest waiting for them!

As they sowed into the river, it carried their seed into their "future," so they continually had a harvest waiting for them. The more we sow, the more we reap, and in turn the more we have to sow. That's God's system for increase!

Another interesting truth we see in Mark 4 and Ecclesiastes 11 is that the harvest is dependent on seed *and* ground. In Mark, even though the seed was sown, the fruit and increase depended upon the seed being sown in *good* ground. Ecclesiastes 11:1 says, "Cast thy bread upon the waters: for thou shalt find it after many days." The picture here is sowing into *moving* waters. Often in Scripture, moving waters are a picture of the moving of the Spirit of God. It appears the best places for increase are where the Spirit of God is moving.

The Windows of Heaven

How do we tap into God's financial system? It starts with the tithe:

MALACHI 3:10
10 Bring ye all the TITHES into the STORE-HOUSE, that there may be meat in mine house, and PROVE ME now herewith, saith the Lord of hosts, if I will not open you the WINDOWS OF HEAVEN, and pour you out a blessing, that there shall not be room enough to receive it.

God said He would open the windows of heaven for those who tithe.

"I can't afford to tithe."

Brother, you can't afford *not* to!

Whatever our income, the first 10 percent goes to the Lord. We don't have to pray about it, we don't have to feel led, and we don't need to see a burning bush in order to tithe. No, we just take the first 10 percent and bring it to the storehouse, which is the local church. The first 10 percent is considered the "firstfruits," or the best part. We are to give God our best, not our leftovers.

Other people say, "I don't have anything left to tithe."

That is why the tithe is called the *first*fruits. If we tithe the first, we won't have that problem.

In the Book of Genesis, God opened the windows of heaven and flooded the whole Earth (Genesis 7:11,12). God is saying to all of us who will tithe, He will open the windows of heaven and flood us with blessings we won't have room to contain! If the first tenth will do that, can you imagine what will happen if we give over and above 10 percent?

Bought and Paid For

God's system of prosperity doesn't work *just* because we do all the right things. It works because Jesus bought and paid for it. For years we've thought we owed God. We thought we were tithing and giving offerings to pay God what we owed. I like to think of it this way: We are not giving out of debt; we are giving out of investment. Jesus paid our debts when He went to the cross. He took the handwriting of ordinances that was against us and nailed it to the cross, according to Colossians 2:14. We couldn't have paid our debts even if we had wanted to! It took Jesus and the plan of redemption to do that. Prosperity is a redemptive blessing, as we see in Deuteronomy 28 and the following scriptures.

2 CORINTHIANS 8:9
9   For ye know the grace of our Lord Jesus Christ, that, though he was rich, yet for your sakes he became poor, that ye through his poverty might be rich.

GALATIANS 3:13
13 Christ hath redeemed us from the curse of the law, being made a curse for us: for it is written, Cursed is every one that hangeth on a tree.

So we give to invest in God's work down here. Like any investment, we need to give it much more than He needs to receive it. A revelation of that makes it possible for our giving to be even more cheerful and with greater anticipation.

Every month most of us have some sort of bill that comes due, whether it be a utility bill or a credit card bill. Every month we write the check and go to the mailbox to send the payment of what we owe that particular company. I have never seen anyone go to pay his bills and jump, shout, and dance and say, "I can't wait to see what I am going to get out of this! I can't wait to see what comes next month." The only thing that is going to come next month is another bill!

No, we are just paying what we owe, and we don't *expect* anything in return. But if someone offered us an investment guaranteed to bring a great return, we would send the check with great joy and anticipation.

In the Old Testament, people paid tithes because they owed God. No one had come and paid their debts yet, so in the Old Testament, giving was out of debt. However, when we get over to the New Testament, Jesus paid our debts! Now the only thing we owe God is our lives. Financially we are not in debt to God, so in the New Testament, giving is not out of debt; it is out of investment!

God's system offers us an investment opportunity that hasn't failed in thousands of years. In the world system we may be thankful to see a 3 percent or even a 5 percent return on our investment. But God's system pays back a *many*fold return! God's system is good measure, pressed down, shaken together, and running over!

You Can't Out-Give God

Growing up, I always heard the phrase, "You can't out-give God!" Even at a time in my life when I wasn't serving God, I was sure to put my tithe in that envelope they gave us at church and save it until I did attend. So tithing and giving were instilled in me at a young age.

I remember going to a Full Gospel Business Men's meeting years ago, shortly after I was saved. The speaker shared how God had led him to do large-scale youth crusades in major cities around the nation. At the meeting he told us, "I feel like we shouldn't expect the youth to pay the bills. I believe God wants the church to pay the bills to reach out to these young people. The Holy Ghost told me there are 12 businessmen here today who are going to give $1,000 each toward financing this project."

I laughed inside and thought, *I don't know where I could borrow that much money right now.*

What the speaker said next surprised me. He said, "Some of you don't even know where you could borrow that much money."

Then I remembered how I had recently been talking to God about the fact that if things didn't change at my job, I was going to have to find another one. I was in the real estate business, working strictly on commission, and my sales had been very low.

The speaker said, "Some of your businesses are doing so badly, you've been talking to God about changing jobs."

At this point I looked down at my hands, which were glued to the arms of the chair. I was holding on so tightly, my knuckles were turning white. I couldn't help thinking, *God, don't do this to me. I don't have any money coming in, and I only have $150 left to my name. How can I give what I don't have?*

The speaker preached on, and no one moved. Everyone sat still as he waited for people to come and give those $1,000 offerings. Then the speaker said, "Some of you don't have $1,000, but if you will come up here and make a pledge, God will honor it."

Before long I found myself getting up and walking toward the front. All the while I was thinking, *O dear God, which way is the door?* I felt dumb. I was the only one going up there, and surely everyone could tell I was broke. They were probably thinking, *That poor kid is just acting on emotions.*

I walked up to the front where the speaker was standing and said, "I don't have any money."

He answered, "That's all right. God will bring it in."

I said, "Well, He is going to have to, because I don't have any now."

I guess seeing me, just a kid compared to everyone else who was there, walk to the front must have shamed some of the businessmen, because when I turned around, a row of men was standing behind me.

I stood there and said, "All right, Lord, I'll write a check for $100 and expect You to bring in the money. Any time a commission check comes in, I will take out what I need to live and send in the rest until that $1,000 pledge is fulfilled."

Giving by Faith

It's amazing the things that one act set into motion in my life. I found out I could give *in* faith, and I could give *by* faith. Giving in faith is when we give and believe God for a return on our seed. Giving by faith is when we don't have the money, but we make a faith promise between God and ourselves. We don't have the money in our hands, but we say, "God, You bring it in and I will give it." It is not writing a check, sending it in, and hoping God will put the money in the account before the check clears. No, giving by faith is when we say, "God, I commit in my heart to give. My heart is willing. Now You bring the money in, and I will give it."

That act of faith broke things loose in the financial realm as well as a lot of other areas in my life. Within 45 days that $1,000 was paid off, my business started increasing, and there was joy in my heart. Soon I was looking for places to give money. I thought, *I like this system!* It's true, you can't out-give God!

There is something about investing in God's system that will cause us to increase beyond what we could even ask or think. Tithing gets the windows of heaven open for a blessing we can't contain, and giving offerings goes even beyond that.

> **2 CORINTHIANS 9:10**
> **10 Now he that ministereth seed to the sower both minister bread for your food, and MULTIPLY YOUR SEED SOWN, and increase the fruits of your righteousness.**

The Bible said God would not only provide us with seed to sow, but He would "...multiply your [resources for] sowing, and increase the fruits of your righteousness [which manifests itself in active goodness, kindness, and charity]" (*The Amplified Bible*). Giving to God is not just a one-way street. Not only do we give, but we receive something in return.

Giving and Receiving

Paul had a good understanding of the benefits of giving and receiving.

> **PHILIPPIANS 4:15-17**
> **15 Now ye Philippians know also, that in the beginning of the gospel, when I departed from Macedonia, no church communicated with me as concerning GIVING and RECEIVING, but ye only.**
> **16 For even in Thessalonica ye sent once and again unto my necessity.**
> **17 Not because I desire a gift: but I desire FRUIT that may ABOUND TO YOUR ACCOUNT.**

Paul's motivation in having the Philippians give was not for his own sake, but for their sake. Any time God tells us to give, it's not to take something *from* us; it's to get something *to* us.

As someone said, "If God puts His hand in your pocket, it's not to take something out; it's to put something in!" Giving is not for His sake, but for ours. If He asks us for something, it's so that He can use it, multiply it, and then put it back in our pocket along with the increase!

The Miracle Is in the House

Someone will say, "Yes, but I don't have anything to give." I guarantee you do. It's not what you don't have to give; it's what you do have. It's not how large or small your seed may be; it's the miracle of what God can do with that seed when it is sown. In the Book of Mark, Jesus said the mustard seed is the least of all seeds, but when it is *sown* it becomes the greatest among herbs (Mark 4:31,32).

Second Corinthians 8:12 says, "For if there be first a willing mind, it is accepted according to that a man hath, and not according to that he hath not."

For example, consider the widow in Second Kings 4:

2 KINGS 4:1
1 Now there cried a certain woman of the wives of the sons of the prophets unto Elisha, saying, Thy servant my husband is dead; and thou knowest that thy servant did fear the Lord: and the creditor is come to take unto him my two sons to be bondmen.

The woman's husband had died, leaving her with debts she had no means of paying, so the bill collector was on his way to take her sons away as slaves. I like what the prophet Elisha asked the woman:

2 KINGS 4:2
2 And Elisha said unto her, What shall I do for thee? tell me, WHAT HAST THOU IN THE HOUSE?

**And she said, Thine handmaid hath not any thing
in the house, save a pot of oil.**

The prophet Elisha asked the woman what she *had*
in her house. The miracle is always in the house! We
may have a need, but I guarantee we also have the
seed. In Second Kings 4:3, Elisha told the woman to
borrow all the vessels she could find. So she sent her
two boys out asking for vessels. She gathered the
vessels together and started pouring the oil into them.
She poured and poured, and the oil didn't stop. Every
time she found another vessel, she kept pouring, and
the oil kept coming out. Then Elisha told her to take
the oil, sell it to pay off her debts, and live off the rest.

Do you know when the oil ran out? When the
woman ran out of vessels. In other words, her lifestyle
was not determined by what God was able to do; it was
determined by what she could believe for. If she would
have borrowed more vessels, the oil would have kept
running until she filled the last one. God said, "I will
keep pouring as long as you give Me places to pour."

The Boy's Lunch

Now let's look for an example in the New Testament.
In John 6, a great multitude came to Jesus as He sat
with His disciples on a mountainside. The multitude
grew hungry, so Jesus asked Philip, "...Whence shall we
buy bread, that these may eat?" (John 6:5).

JOHN 6:7-9
**7 Philip answered him, Two hundred pennyworth
of bread is not sufficient for them, that every one
of them may take a little.**
**8 One of his disciples, Andrew, Simon Peter's
brother, saith unto him,**

9 There is a lad here, which hath five barley loaves, and two small fishes: but what are they among so many?

There was a great need — the Bible tells us this was a crowd of 5,000 people! Jesus asked His disciples how the people were going to be fed, and their response was, "We don't have enough money with us to buy food to give even a little to each person."

Luke's account of this tells us what Jesus had been teaching His disciples. Luke 9:11 says, "And the people, when they knew it, followed him: and he received them, and spake unto them of the kingdom of God...."

To walk in the blessings of the kingdom of God, we need to understand how the kingdom of God operates. How does it operate?

> **MARK 4:26,28,30-32**
> **26 ...So is the kingdom of God, as if a man should cast seed into the ground...**
> **28 For the earth bringeth forth fruit of herself; first the blade, then the ear, after that the full corn in the ear...**
> **30 And he said, Whereunto shall we liken the kingdom of God? or with what comparison shall we compare it?**
> **31 It is like a grain of mustard seed, which, when it is sown in the earth, is less than all the seeds that be in the earth:**
> **32 But when it is sown, it groweth up, and becometh greater than all herbs, and shooteth out great branches; so that the fowls of the air may lodge under the shadow of it.**

The disciples had been with Jesus, witnessed His miracles, and heard this message, but they still didn't "catch" it. The 5,000 waiting to be fed had heard the same message, and they didn't "catch" it. However, there was a young boy in the crowd who did! He had a lunch of five barley loaves and two small fishes. He took it to the disciples and sowed what he had.

In essence, the boy was saying, "The kingdom of God operates on sowing and reaping. Do you need a miracle, a harvest, or an increase? Here, I have a seed." Simon Peter presented the loaves and fishes to Jesus, saying, "...what are they among so many?" (John 6:9).

> **JOHN 6:10,11**
> **10 And Jesus said, Make the men sit down. Now there was much grass in the place. So the men sat down, in number about five thousand.**
> **11 And Jesus took the loaves; and when he had given thanks, he distributed to the disciples, and the disciples to them that were set down; and likewise of the fishes as much as they would.**

I've heard people say, "You must understand, loaves were bigger in those days than they are now."

If that's the case, that little boy must have had quite an appetite!

I've also heard, "Everybody got just a little bit." That's not what the Bible says.

> **JOHN 6:12,13**
> **12 When they were FILLED, he said unto his disciples, Gather up the FRAGMENTS THAT REMAIN, that nothing be lost.**
> **13 Therefore they gathered them together, and filled twelve baskets with the fragments of the five barley loaves, which remained over and above unto them that had eaten.**

One thing to realize about Jesus: He isn't extravagant, nor is He wasteful. There was enough for everyone to eat until they were filled and had 12 baskets left over. Who do you suppose took the 12 baskets home? I wouldn't be surprised if it was that little boy!

The boy didn't have much to offer — only five loaves and two fishes — but he took it to the disciples, and they gave it to Jesus. Jesus took a little boy's lunch, blessed it, broke it, and handed it to His disciples. They fed 5,000 people, and after everyone was full, they gathered up 12 baskets full.

Peter's Boat

People have said, "You talk about sowing seeds and the great blessings that will come, but I don't have anything to give." The key is to start with what you do have, no matter how small it may seem, and let God give the increase.

In Luke 5, Jesus was walking along and came across a crowd of people near the Lake of Gennesaret who were hungry to hear the Word of God. Jesus couldn't minister to them from where He was, but He saw "...two ships standing by the lake: but the fishermen were gone out of them, and were washing their nets" (Luke 5:2).

Jesus approached one of the men, who happened to be Simon Peter, and asked him to take his boat out a little distance from the shore so Jesus could teach the people from there. After Jesus finished teaching the people, He turned His attention back to Simon Peter.

> **LUKE 5:4-7**
> **4 Now when he had left speaking, he said unto Simon, Launch out into the deep, and let down your nets for a draught.**
> **5 And Simon answering said unto him, Master, we have TOILED ALL THE NIGHT, and have TAKEN**

NOTHING: nevertheless at thy word I will let down the net.
6 And when they had this done, they inclosed a GREAT MULTITUDE of fishes: and their net brake.
7 And they beckoned unto their PARTNERS, which were in the other ship, that they should come and help them. And they came, and filled both the ships, so that they began to sink.

What did Peter have to offer Jesus? Nothing but a failing fishing business. His out-go was more than his income. He had fished all night, taken nothing, and now had to spend time washing his nets. Peter gave the only thing he could offer, his empty boat, for Jesus to minister to the multitude.

It's not just what we have to give; it's the obedience with which we give. No matter what it is, God will use it to bless people and multiply it back to us. After Jesus had used the boat to spiritually feed the multitude, He filled it with so many fish, it almost sank Peter's boat *and* his partner's.

The Widow's Mite

The widow in Mark 12 is an example of the attitude with which we should give:

MARK 12:41-44
41 And Jesus sat over against the treasury, and beheld how the people cast money into the treasury: and MANY THAT WERE RICH CAST IN MUCH.
42 And there came a certain poor widow, and she threw in TWO MITES, which make a farthing.
43 And he called unto him his disciples, and saith unto them, Verily I say unto you, That THIS POOR WIDOW HATH CAST MORE IN, than all they which have cast into the treasury:

**44 For all they did cast in OF THEIR ABUNDANCE;
BUT SHE OF HER WANT did cast in ALL THAT
SHE HAD, even all her living.**

Sometimes God's view of the size of our seed or gift
is determined not by how much we give, but by what we
have left after we give. Compared to the amount the
rich people gave, the widow's two mites may have
seemed insignificant, but to God she gave more than all
the rich people, because she gave all she had.

Sowing Two Seeds

There is another part to prosperity we need to
understand. If we think prosperity is going to work
through giving alone, we could get ourselves into
trouble. If prosperity operated on giving alone, it would
be based strictly on our works. That would be considered
Old Covenant or Law, but thank God, we don't live
under the Old Covenant. Thank God, we live under the
New Covenant.

In the New Covenant, we live under *grace*. And grace
works by faith, which is basically believing and saying.
So we could say prosperity works by two principles:
sowing, which is activating our faith, and *saying*, which
is releasing our faith. Think about how we received
salvation.

ROMANS 10:9,10
**9   That if thou shalt CONFESS WITH THY MOUTH
the Lord Jesus, and shalt believe in thine heart
that God hath raised him from the dead, thou shalt
be saved.**
**10 For with the heart man believeth unto
righteousness; and WITH THE MOUTH CONFES-
SION is made unto salvation.**

Our confession, or what we say, seems to have something to do with what we believe. Paul said in Second Corinthians 4:13, "We having the same spirit of faith, according as it is written, I believed, and therefore have I spoken; we also believe, and therefore speak."

It seems we have understood the *sowing* part. We put our tithes and offerings in the offering plate faithfully, and that is wonderful; but it seems we have been missing it in the *saying* part. It doesn't do much good to plant our seed and then pull it out of the ground with our words.

I learned this lesson when Janet and I began to travel. Our first trip took us to Arizona, Texas, and Oklahoma. By the time we had finished our last meeting, we had just enough money to put aside for our expenses. We paid our bills and had nothing left. Our next scheduled meeting was in Michigan, nearly 950 miles away. Our gas tank was empty, and we had no money to fill the tank.

At that point, I said to the Lord, "God, you called me. You said a man's gift will make room for him, so Lord, You have to get me to the room!" Supernaturally, someone walked up to me the night before we were to leave and placed some money in my pocket. That bill was enough to fill our gas tank and pay our way to the next meeting.

Up until this point, things didn't look very good for us in the natural. We had meetings where people stayed away by the hundreds. Our offerings were small. It looked as if we were going nowhere fast. But there is something about lining your mouth up with what the Bible says.

I had an opportunity to do a lot of thinking on that drive to Michigan. I kept meditating on Philippians

4:19, "But my God shall supply all your [my] need according to his riches in glory by Christ Jesus," and Mark 11:23, "...whosoever shall say..., he shall have whatsoever he saith...." Those two scriptures kept rolling around inside me. You have to be full of the Word before you can say anything. After meditating on these verses for several hours, I turned to Janet and said, "From this day forward we will never again lack for a place to preach. We will never lack for vehicles. We will never lack for finances to do the will of God."

I didn't feel anything. I didn't have to feel anything. I just lined my mouth up with what the Word of God says. Prosperity isn't going to come from giving alone. When we sow, we're going to have to learn to mix faith with our giving. We need to learn to line up our *saying* with our *sowing*.

Prosperity Through the Word

How does faith come? Romans 10:17 says, "So then faith cometh by hearing, and hearing by the word of God." Just like faith, true Bible prosperity comes through the Word of God.

As we read earlier, the Bible says, "Beloved, I wish above all things that thou mayest prosper and be in health, even as thy soul prospereth" (3 John 2). The only thing that will prosper our souls is the Word of God. No one is more prosperous than the one who walks in the Word of God. Notice what the first Psalm says:

PSALM 1:1-3
1 BLESSED IS THE MAN that walketh not in the counsel of the ungodly, nor standeth in the way of sinners, nor sitteth in the seat of the scornful.

> **2 But his delight is in THE LAW OF THE LORD; and IN HIS LAW doth he MEDIATE DAY AND NIGHT.**
> **3 And he shall be like a tree planted by the rivers of water, that bringeth forth his fruit in his season; his leaf also shall not wither; and WHATSOEVER HE DOETH SHALL PROSPER.**

The man whose delight is in the law of the Lord, or the Word of God, will be prosperous in whatever he does. Prosperity comes as a result of feeding on God's Word and walking in His will.

Joshua 1:8 gives us the same instructions.

> **JOSHUA 1:8**
> **8 This BOOK OF THE LAW shall not depart OUT OF THY MOUTH; but thou shalt MEDITATE therein DAY AND NIGHT, that thou mayest observe to do according to all that is written therein: for then thou shalt make thy way PROSPEROUS, and then thou shalt have good success.**

In other words, mediate on the Word of God and keep speaking it day and night. To meditate means to "mutter" or to speak quietly to oneself. The *James Moffatt* translation says, "...This lawbook you shall never cease to have on your lips...."

Psalm 35:27 says, "Let them shout for joy, and be glad, that favour my righteous cause: yea, let them *say continually*, Let the Lord be magnified, which hath pleasure in the prosperity of his servant."

If we are saying *continually* that God takes pleasure in our prosperity, there is no room to say, "I'm broke, and nothing ever works for me."

Accessing Your Heavenly Account

Every time we sow into the work of God by bringing our tithes, giving offerings, and obeying God when He tells us to give, God credits our "heavenly account." Let's look at what the Word of God has to say about our heavenly account. In Mark 10, Jesus was talking to the rich young ruler and said:

> **MARK 10:21**
> **21 ...One thing thou lackest: go thy way, sell whatsoever thou hast, and give to the poor, and thou shalt have TREASURE IN HEAVEN....**

Jesus didn't say it was wrong for the man to have money. The problem was that the money was standing between the man and his relationship with God. Instructing the man to give all his belongings away was not God's way of trying to take the man from riches to poverty; it was God's way of transferring the man from an *earthly* account to a *heavenly* account. Jesus told the man, "You will have *treasure in heaven* if you give what you have and follow Me."

If we stop and think about it, why would heaven need our treasure? On the Earth, we think gold is great. In heaven, God uses gold for pavement! Heaven doesn't need our treasure, and we are not laying up treasure for when we are in heaven. There is enough in heaven already.

> **MATTHEW 6:19-21**
> **19 Lay not up for yourselves treasures upon earth, where moth and rust doth corrupt, and where thieves break through and steal:**
> **20 But lay up for yourselves treasures in heaven, where neither moth nor rust doth corrupt, and where thieves do not break through nor steal:**

21 For where your treasure is, there will your heart be also.

God has a heavenly account that we access and operate from the Earth. Why? Because every time we give, it is considered an investment into lives. We may have thought our tithe was going to our church, or our offerings were going to certain individuals, but God said every time we give, it goes into our heavenly account.

How do we access our heavenly account? Every time we give, our seed is multiplied, and our heavenly account draws interest. Our heavenly account has been growing for years, but we have locked the doors to our heavenly account with our mouth. *Sowing* puts the money into our account, and *saying* takes it out of our account.

Someone will say, "Brother, I have been giving for years, and it has never worked for me." That statement shows me why it's not working. If we change what we are saying, I guarantee things will change for us. We should never lock the doors to our heavenly account with our lips. Let's obey God, give when He says to give, and keep our words lined up with our giving. That is how we access our heavenly account.

Sow It, Say It, See It

Our words add faith to our seed. Faith works by believing and saying. In Mark 11, Jesus was teaching on faith, and He included the importance of what we say:

MARK 11:22,23
22 And Jesus answering saith unto them, Have faith in God.
23 For verily I say unto you, That whosoever shall SAY unto this mountain, Be thou removed, and be thou cast into the sea; and shall not doubt in his

heart, but shall believe that those things which he SAITH shall come to pass; he shall have whatsoever he SAITH.

Many people have sown great amounts into the kingdom of God and then negated everything with their words. If we want to see the blessings of God, it is going to take *sowing* in obedience to God and *saying* in line with His Word.

When we are full of the Word, we won't be able to say anything but, "...my God shall supply all your need according to his riches in glory by Christ Jesus" (Philippians 4:19), and "Christ hath redeemed us from the curse of the law..." (Galatians 3:13).

If we can't *talk* poverty, we won't *walk* poverty!

If we are faithful to obey God and get our mouth hooked up with our sowing, payday will come. It may not come every Friday, but it always comes. God has a system for increase, and when we step into it, there is no limit to what He will do!

God's Final Harvest

Great prosperity is coming to the Church in these last days. God has a harvest account reserved for the Church, and it is about to be loosed into our hands to finance the last and greatest move of God on the Earth. The Bible tells us, "...the abundance of the sea shall be converted unto thee, the forces [or wealth] of the Gentiles shall come unto thee" (Isaiah 60:5).

The money is already in the Earth, placed here by God from the foundations of the world. It has been in the world system, being heaped up and stockpiled to be used for the last days. Now a great transfer is about to take place! Proverbs 13:22 tells us, "...the wealth of the sinner [finds its way eventually] into the hands of the righteous, for whom it was laid up" (*Amp*).

The money isn't coming to everyone in the Church, however. It's coming to those who know how to operate in God's financial system. It's coming to those who understand what the money is to be used for. Financial prosperity will come to those who pray and know how to operate God's principles of sowing and reaping where money is concerned.

We are living in the days of the Book of Acts, where they prayed, power flowed, and finances flooded the Church. It's time for the Church to pray like we have never prayed before. "...The earnest (heartfelt, continued) prayer of a righteous man makes tremendous power available — dynamic in its working." Our prayers will bring mighty demonstrations of God's power to Earth, poured out in the way of signs, wonders, and miracles. This power will usher in a flood of prosperity which will help sweep God's final harvest into the barns.

It's coming! We're right on the edge of it! The door to the greatest move of God this Earth has ever seen is about to open. Prayer, power, and prosperity are the three keys that will unlock that door!

CHAPTER 7
Prosperity Scriptures

There is a flood of prosperity coming to God's people. But in order for God to channel the money *through* us, He first has to get it *to* us. God's system for prosperity is not an instant, get-rich-quick scheme. It is a lifestyle of tithing, sowing seed, believing in line with God's Word, and speaking His Word out of our mouths.

The following scriptures are God's Word concerning prosperity. Meditate on them. Plant them in your heart. Speak them out of your mouth until prosperity becomes your lifestyle.

3 JOHN 2
2   Beloved, I wish above all things that thou mayest prosper and be in health, even as thy soul prospereth.

2 CORINTHIANS 9:8
8   And God is able to make all grace abound toward you; that ye, always having all sufficiency in all things, may abound to every good work.

2 CORINTHIANS 9:8 (*Amp*)
8   And God is able to make all grace (every favor and earthly blessing) come to you in abundance, so that you may always and under all circumstances and whatever the need, be self-sufficient — possessing enough to require no aid or support and furnished in abundance for every good work and charitable donation.

GENESIS 12:1-3

1   Now the Lord had said unto Abram, Get thee out of thy country, and from thy kindred, and from thy father's house, unto a land that I will shew thee:

2   And I will make of thee a great nation, and I will bless thee, and make thy name great; and thou shalt be a blessing:

3   And I will bless them that bless thee, and curse him that curseth thee: and in thee shall all families of the earth be blessed.

GENESIS 17:5-7

5   Neither shall thy name any more be called Abram, but thy name shall be Abraham; for a father of many nations have I made thee.

6   And I will make thee exceeding fruitful, and I will make nations of thee, and kings shall come out of thee.

7   And I will establish my covenant between me and thee and thy seed after thee in their generations for an everlasting covenant, to be a God unto thee, and to thy seed after thee.

GALATIANS 3:13,14

13 Christ hath redeemed us from the curse of the law, being made a curse for us: for it is written, Cursed is every one that hangeth on a tree:

14 That the blessing of Abraham might come on the Gentiles through Jesus Christ; that we might receive the promise of the Spirit through faith.

GALATIANS 3:29

29 And if ye be Christ's, then are ye Abraham's seed, and heirs according to the promise.

GALATIANS 3:9

9   So then they which be of faith are blessed with faithful Abraham.

PROVERBS 3:9,10

9 Honour the Lord with thy substance, and with the firstfruits of all thine increase:

10 So shall thy barns be filled with plenty, and thy presses shall burst out with new wine.

MALACHI 3:10

10 Bring ye all the tithes into the storehouse, that there may be meat in mine house, and prove me now herewith, saith the Lord of hosts, if I will not open you the windows of heaven, and pour you out a blessing, that there shall not be room enough to receive it.

GENESIS 8:22

22 While the earth remaineth, seedtime and harvest, and cold and heat, and summer and winter, and day and night shall not cease.

GALATIANS 6:7

7 Be not deceived; God is not mocked: for whatsoever a man soweth, that shall he also reap.

1 CORINTHIANS 3:6

6 I have planted, Apollos watered; but God gave the increase.

ECCLESIASTES 11:1

1 Cast thy bread upon the waters: for thou shalt find it after many days.

ISAIAH 55:10

10 For as the rain cometh down, and the snow from heaven, and returneth not thither, but watereth the earth, and maketh it bring forth and bud, that it may give seed to the sower, and bread to the eater.

2 CORINTHIANS 9:10

10 Now he that ministereth seed to the sower both minister bread for your food, and multiply your seed sown, and increase the fruits of your righteousness.

MARK 4:8

8   And other fell on good ground, and did yield fruit that sprang up and increased; and brought forth, some thirty, and some sixty, and some an hundred.

ISAIAH 1:19

19 If ye be willing and obedient, ye shall eat the good of the land:

ISAIAH 1:19 (*The Living Bible*)

19 If you will only let me help you, if you will only obey, then I will make you rich!

MARK 4:23-29

23 If any man have ears to hear, let him hear.

24 And he said unto them, Take heed what ye hear: with what measure ye mete, it shall be measured to you: and unto you that hear shall more be given.

25 For he that hath, to him shall be given: and he that hath not, from him shall be taken even that which he hath.

26 And he said, So is the kingdom of God, as if a man should cast seed into the ground;

27 And should sleep, and rise night and day, and the seed should spring and grow up, he knoweth not how.

28 For the earth bringeth forth fruit of herself; first the blade, then the ear, after that the full corn in the ear.

29 But when the fruit is brought forth, immediately he putteth in the sickle, because the harvest is come.

GENESIS 39:2,3

2   And the Lord was with Joseph, and he was a prosperous man; and he was in the house of his master the Egyptian.

3   And his master saw that the Lord was with him, and that the Lord made all that he did to prosper in his hand.

MARK 11:23,24

23   For verily I say unto you, That whosoever shall say unto this mountain, Be thou removed, and be thou cast into the sea; and shall not doubt in his heart, but shall believe that those things which he saith shall come to pass; he shall have whatsoever he saith.

24   Therefore I say unto you, What things soever ye desire, when ye pray, believe that ye receive them, and ye shall have them.

JOSHUA 1:8

8   This book of the law shall not depart out of thy mouth; but thou shalt meditate therein day and night, that thou mayest observe to do according to all that is written therein: for then thou shalt make thy way prosperous, and then thou shalt have good success.

PSALM 1:1-3

1   Blessed is the man that walketh not in the counsel of the ungodly, nor standeth in the way of sinners, nor sitteth in the seat of the scornful.

2   But his delight is in the law of the Lord; and in his law doth he meditate day and night.

3   And he shall be like a tree planted by the rivers of water, that bringeth forth his fruit in his season; his leaf also shall not wither; and whatsoever he doeth shall prosper.

DEUTERONOMY 8:6-9

6 Therefore thou shalt keep the commandments of the Lord thy God, to walk in his ways, and to fear him.

7 For the Lord thy God bringeth thee into a good land, a land of brooks of water, of fountains and depths that spring out of valleys and hills;

8 A land of wheat, and barley, and vines, and fig trees, and pomegranates; a land of oil olive, and honey;

9 A land wherein thou shalt eat bread without scarceness, thou shalt not lack any thing in it; a land whose stones are iron, and out of whose hills thou mayest dig brass.

DEUTERONOMY 8:18

18 But thou shalt remember the Lord thy God: for it is he that giveth thee power to get wealth, that he may establish his covenant which he sware unto thy fathers, as it is this day.

DEUTERONOMY 29:9

9 Keep therefore the words of this covenant, and do them, that ye may prosper in all that ye do.

PSALM 118: 25

25 Save now, I beseech thee, O Lord: O Lord, I beseech thee, send now prosperity.

PSALM 84:11

11 For the Lord God is a sun and shield: the Lord will give grace and glory: no good thing will he withhold from them that walk uprightly.

JOHN 4:36

36 And he that reapeth receiveth wages, and gathereth fruit unto life eternal: that both he that soweth and he that reapeth may rejoice together.

ISAIAH 60:1-5

1   Arise, shine; for thy light is come, and the glory of the Lord is risen upon thee.

2   For, behold, the darkness shall cover the earth, and gross darkness the people: but the Lord shall arise upon thee, and his glory shall be seen upon thee.

3   And the Gentiles shall come to thy light, and kings to the brightness of thy rising.

4   Lift up thine eyes round about, and see: all they gather themselves together, they come to thee: thy sons shall come from far, and thy daughters shall be nursed at thy side.

5   Then thou shalt see, and flow together, and thine heart shall fear, and be enlarged; because the abundance of the sea shall be converted unto thee, the forces [wealth] of the Gentiles shall come unto thee.

JOB 27:16,17

16 Though he heap up silver as the dust, and prepare raiment as the clay;

17 He may prepare it, but the just shall put it on, and the innocent shall divide the silver.

PROVERBS 13:22

22 A good man leaveth an inheritance to his children's children: and the wealth of the sinner is laid up for the just.

ECCLESIASTES 2:26

26 For God giveth to a man that is good in his sight wisdom, and knowledge, and joy: but to the sinner he giveth travail, to gather and to heap up, that he may give to him that is good before God....

PSALM 113:7,8

7 He raiseth up the poor out of the dust, and lifteth the needy out of the dunghill;

8 That he may set him with princes, even with the princes of his people.

PROVERBS 28:20

20 A faithful man shall abound with blessings: but he that maketh haste to be rich shall not be innocent.

PROVERBS 22:4

4 By humility and the fear of the Lord are riches, and honour, and life.

ISAIAH 45:3

3 And I will give thee the treasures of darkness, and hidden riches of secret places, that thou mayest know that I, the Lord, which call thee by thy name, am the God of Israel.

HAGGAI 2:7-9

7 And I will shake all nations, and the desire of all nations shall come: and I will fill this house with glory, saith the Lord of hosts.

8 The silver is mine, and the gold is mine, saith the Lord of hosts.

9 The glory of this latter house shall be greater than of the former, saith the Lord of hosts: and in this place will I give peace, saith the Lord of hosts.

PSALM 68:19

19 Blessed be the Lord, who daily loadeth us with benefits, even the God of our salvation. Selah.

PROVERBS 22:9

9 He that hath a bountiful eye shall be blessed; for he giveth of his bread to the poor.

PROVERBS 19:17

17 He that hath pity upon the poor lendeth unto the Lord; and that which he hath given will he pay him again.

LUKE 6:38

38 Give, and it shall be given unto you; good measure, pressed down, and shaken together, and running over, shall men give into your bosom. For with the same measure that ye mete withal it shall be measured to you again.

2 CORINTHIANS 9:6

6 But this I say, He which soweth sparingly shall reap also sparingly; and he which soweth bountifully shall reap also bountifully.

PROVERBS 11:24,25

24 There is that scattereth, and yet increaseth; and there is that withholdeth more than is meet, but it tendeth to poverty.
25 The liberal soul shall be made fat: and he that watereth shall be watered also himself.

PSALM 5:12

12 For thou, Lord, wilt bless the righteous; with favour wilt thou compass him as with a shield.

PSALM 34:9,10

9 O fear the Lord, ye his saints: for there is no want to them that fear him.
10 The young lions do lack, and suffer hunger: but they that seek the Lord shall not want any good thing.

PSALM 37:21

21 The wicked borroweth, and payeth not again: but the righteous sheweth mercy, and giveth.

PROVERBS 10:22
22 The blessing of the Lord, it maketh rich, and he addeth no sorrow with it.

PSALM 23:1-6
1   The Lord is my shepherd; I shall not want.
2   He maketh me to lie down in green pastures: he leadeth me beside the still waters.
3   He restoreth my soul: he leadeth me in the paths of righteousness for his name's sake.
4   Yea, though I walk through the valley of the shadow of death, I will fear no evil: for thou art with me; thy rod and thy staff they comfort me.
5   Thou preparest a table before me in the presence of mine enemies: thou anointest my head with oil; my cup runneth over.
6   Surely goodness and mercy shall follow me all the days of my life: and I will dwell in the house of the Lord for ever.

2 CORINTHIANS 8:9
9   For ye know the grace of our Lord Jesus Christ, that, though he was rich, yet for your sakes he became poor, that ye through his poverty might be rich.

1 TIMOTHY 6:17
17 Charge them that are rich in this world, that they be not highminded, nor trust in uncertain riches, but in the living God, who giveth us richly all things to enjoy.

MATTHEW 6:19-21
19 Lay not up for yourselves treasures upon earth, where moth and rust doth corrupt, and where thieves break through and steal:
20 But lay up for yourselves treasures in heaven, where neither moth nor rust doth corrupt, and where thieves do not break through nor steal:
21 For where your treasure is, there will your heart be also.

MATTHEW 6:33

33 But seek ye first the kingdom of God, and his righteousness; and all these things shall be added unto you.

PHILIPPIANS 4:19

19 But my God shall supply all your need according to his riches in glory by Christ Jesus.

PSALM 35:27

27 Let them shout for joy, and be glad, that favour my righteous cause: yea, let them say continually, Let the Lord be magnified, which hath pleasure in the prosperity of his servant.